The Department of the Air Force

The Department of the Air Force

John Rhea

CHELSEA HOUSE PUBLISHERS

On the cover: A 1974 view of a YF-16 supersonic fighter in a 100-degree climb over Edwards Air Force Base in California.
Frontispiece: A reenactment of a World War I dogfight.

CHELSEA HOUSE PUBLISHERS
Editor-in-Chief: Nancy Toff
Executive Editor: Remmel T. Nunn
Managing Editor: Karyn Gullen Browne
Copy Chief: Juliann Barbato
Picture Editor: Adrian G. Allen
Art Director: Maria Epes
Manufacturing Manager: Gerald Levine

Know Your Government
Senior Editor: Kathy Kuhtz

Staff for THE DEPARTMENT OF THE AIR FORCE
Assistant Editor: James M. Cornelius
Copy Editor: Brian Sookram
Deputy Copy Chief: Nicole Bowen
Editorial Assistant: Elizabeth Nix
Picture Research: Dixon & Turner Research Associates, Inc.; Joann Stern
Picture Coordinator: Melanie Sanford
Assistant Art Director: Loraine Machlin
Senior Designer: Noreen M. Lamb
Production Manager: Joseph Romano
Production Coordinator: Marie Claire Cebrián

3 5 7 9 8 6 4 2

Library of Congress Cataloging-in-Publication Data

Rhea, John.
   The Department of the Air Force / John Rhea.
      p.   cm. —(Know your government)
   Bibliography: p.
   Includes index.
   ISBN 0-87754-834-X
         0-7910-0884-3 (pbk.)
   1. United States. Dept. of the Air Force.   I. Title.
II. Series: Know your government (New York, N.Y.)
UG633.R45   1990   89-10026
353.63—dc20   CIP

94- 2729
YA
J
358
RHE

CONTENTS

KNOW YOUR GOVERNMENT

The American Red Cross

The Bureau of Indian Affairs

The Central Intelligence Agency

The Commission on Civil Rights

The Department of Agriculture

The Department of the Air Force

The Department of the Army

The Department of Commerce

The Department of Defense

The Department of Education

The Department of Energy

The Department of Health and
Human Services

The Department of Housing and
Urban Development

The Department of the Interior

The Department of Justice

The Department of Labor

The Department of the Navy

The Department of State

The Department of Transportation

The Department of the Treasury

The Drug Enforcement Administration

The Environmental Protection Agency

The Equal Employment
Opportunities Commission

The Federal Aviation Administration

The Federal Bureau of Investigation

The Federal Communications Commission

The Federal Government: How it Works

The Federal Reserve System

The Federal Trade Commission

The Food and Drug Administration

The Forest Service

The House of Representatives

The Immigration and Naturalization Service

The Internal Revenue Service

The Library of Congress

The National Aeronautics and Space
Administration

The National Archives and Records
Administration

The National Foundation on the Arts
and the Humanities

The National Park Service

The National Science Foundation

The Nuclear Regulatory Commission

The Peace Corps

The Presidency

The Public Health Service

The Securities and Exchange Commission

The Senate

The Small Business Administration

The Smithsonian

The Supreme Court

The Tennessee Valley Authority

The U.S. Arms Control and
Disarmament Agency

The U.S. Coast Guard

The U.S. Constitution

The U.S. Fish and Wildlife Service

The U.S. Information Agency

The U.S. Marine Corps

The U.S. Mint

The U.S. Postal Service

The U.S. Secret Service

The Veterans Administration

CHELSEA HOUSE PUBLISHERS

INTRODUCTION

Government: Crises of Confidence

Arthur M. Schlesinger, jr.

From the start, Americans have regarded their government with a mixture of reliance and mistrust. The men who founded the republic did not doubt the indispensability of government. "If men were angels," observed the 51st Federalist Paper, "no government would be necessary." But men are not angels. Because human beings are subject to wicked as well as to noble impulses, government was deemed essential to assure freedom and order.

At the same time, the American revolutionaries knew that government could also become a source of injury and oppression. The men who gathered in Philadelphia in 1787 to write the Constitution therefore had two purposes in mind. They wanted to establish a strong central authority and to limit that central authority's capacity to abuse its power.

To prevent the abuse of power, the Founding Fathers wrote two basic principles into the new Constitution. The principle of federalism divided power between the state governments and the central authority. The principle of the separation of powers subdivided the central authority itself into three branches—the executive, the legislative, and the judiciary—so that "each may be a check on the other." The *Know Your Government* series focuses on the major executive departments and agencies in these branches of the federal government.

7

The Constitution did not plan the executive branch in any detail. After vesting the executive power in the president, it assumed the existence of "executive departments" without specifying what these departments should be. Congress began defining their functions in 1789 by creating the Departments of State, Treasury, and War. The secretaries in charge of these departments made up President Washington's first cabinet. Congress also provided for a legal officer, and President Washington soon invited the attorney general, as he was called, to attend cabinet meetings. As need required, Congress created more executive departments.

Setting up the cabinet was only the first step in organizing the American state. With almost no guidance from the Constitution, President Washington, seconded by Alexander Hamilton, his brilliant secretary of the treasury, equipped the infant republic with a working administrative structure. The Federalists believed in both executive energy and executive accountability and set high standards for public appointments. The Jeffersonian opposition had less faith in strong government and preferred local government to the central authority. But when Jefferson himself became president in 1801, although he set out to change the direction of policy, he found no reason to alter the framework the Federalists had erected.

By 1801 there were about 3,000 federal civilian employees in a nation of a little more than 5 million people. Growth in territory and population steadily enlarged national responsibilities. Thirty years later, when Jackson was president, there were more than 11,000 government workers in a nation of 13 million. The federal establishment was increasing at a faster rate than the population.

Jackson's presidency brought significant changes in the federal service. He believed that the executive branch contained too many officials who saw their jobs as "species of property" and as "a means of promoting individual interest." Against the idea of a permanent service based on life tenure, Jackson argued for the periodic redistribution of federal offices, contending that this was the democratic way and that official duties could be made "so plain and simple that men of intelligence may readily qualify themselves for their performance." He called this policy rotation-in-office. His opponents called it the spoils system.

In fact, partisan legend exaggerated the extent of Jackson's removals. More than 80 percent of federal officeholders retained their jobs. Jackson discharged no larger a proportion of government workers than Jefferson had done a generation earlier. But the rise in these years of mass political parties gave federal patronage new importance as a means of building the party and of rewarding activists. Jackson's successors were less restrained in the distribu-

8

tion of spoils. As the federal establishment grew—to nearly 40,000 by 1861—the politicization of the public service excited increasing concern.

After the Civil War the spoils system became a major political issue. High-minded men condemned it as the root of all political evil. The spoilsmen, said the British commentator James Bryce, "have distorted and depraved the mechanism of politics." Patronage, by giving jobs to unqualified, incompetent, and dishonest persons, lowered the standards of public service and nourished corrupt political machines. Office-seekers pursued presidents and cabinet secretaries without mercy. "Patronage," said Ulysses S. Grant after his presidency, "is the bane of the presidential office." "Every time I appoint someone to office," said another political leader, "I make a hundred enemies and one ingrate." George William Curtis, the president of the National Civil Service Reform League, summed up the indictment. He said,

> The theory which perverts public trusts into party spoils, making public
> employment dependent upon personal favor and not on proved merit,
> necessarily ruins the self-respect of public employees, destroys the
> function of party in a republic, prostitutes elections into a desperate
> strife for personal profit, and degrades the national character by lower-
> ing the moral tone and standard of the country.

The object of civil service reform was to promote efficiency and honesty in the public service and to bring about the ethical regeneration of public life. Over bitter opposition from politicians, the reformers in 1883 passed the Pendleton Act, establishing a bipartisan Civil Service Commission, competitive examinations, and appointment on merit. The Pendleton Act also gave the president authority to extend by executive order the number of "classified" jobs—that is, jobs subject to the merit system. The act applied initially only to about 14,000 of the more than 100,000 federal positions. But by the end of the 19th century 40 percent of federal jobs had moved into the classified category.

Civil service reform was in part a response to the growing complexity of American life. As society grew more organized and problems more technical, official duties were no longer so plain and simple that any person of intelligence could perform them. In public service, as in other areas, the all-round man was yielding ground to the expert, the amateur to the professional. The excesses of the spoils system thus provoked the counter-ideal of scientific public administration, separate from politics and, as far as possible, insulated against it.

The cult of the expert, however, had its own excesses. The idea that administration could be divorced from policy was an illusion. And in the realm of policy, the expert, however much segregated from partisan politics, can never attain perfect objectivity. He remains the prisoner of his own set of values. It is these values rather than technical expertise that determine fundamental judgments of public policy. To turn over such judgments to experts, moreover, would be to abandon democracy itself; for in a democracy final decisions must be made by the people and their elected representatives. "The business of the expert," the British political scientist Harold Laski rightly said, "is to be on tap and not on top."

Politics, however, were deeply ingrained in American folkways. This meant intermittent tension between the presidential government, elected every four years by the people, and the permanent government, which saw presidents come and go while it went on forever. Sometimes the permanent government knew better than its political masters; sometimes it opposed or sabotaged valuable new initiatives. In the end a strong president with effective cabinet secretaries could make the permanent government responsive to presidential purpose, but it was often an exasperating struggle.

The struggle within the executive branch was less important, however, than the growing impatience with bureaucracy in society as a whole. The 20th century saw a considerable expansion of the federal establishment. The Great Depression and the New Deal led the national government to take on a variety of new responsibilities. The New Deal extended the federal regulatory apparatus. By 1940, in a nation of 130 million people, the number of federal workers for the first time passed the 1 million mark. The Second World War brought federal civilian employment to 3.8 million in 1945. With peace, the federal establishment declined to around 2 million by 1950. Then growth resumed, reaching 2.8 million by the 1980s.

The New Deal years saw rising criticism of "big government" and "bureaucracy." Businessmen resented federal regulation. Conservatives worried about the impact of paternalistic government on individual self-reliance, on community responsibility, and on economic and personal freedom. The nation in effect renewed the old debate between Hamilton and Jefferson in the early republic, although with an ironic exchange of positions. For the Hamiltonian constituency, the "rich and well-born," once the advocate of affirmative government, now condemned government intervention, while the Jeffersonian constituency, the plain people, once the advocate of a weak central government and of states' rights, now favored government intervention.

In the 1980s, with the presidency of Ronald Reagan, the debate has burst out with unusual intensity. According to conservatives, government intervention abridges liberty, stifles enterprise, and is inefficient, wasteful, and

10

arbitrary. It disturbs the harmony of the self-adjusting market and creates worse troubles than it solves. Get government off our backs, according to the popular cliché, and our problems will solve themselves. When government is necessary, let it be at the local level, close to the people. Above all, stop the inexorable growth of the federal government.

In fact, for all the talk about the "swollen" and "bloated" bureaucracy, the federal establishment has not been growing as inexorably as many Americans seem to believe. In 1949, it consisted of 2.1 million people. Thirty years later, while the country had grown by 70 million, the federal force had grown only by 750,000. Federal workers were a smaller percentage of the population in 1985 than they were in 1955—or in 1940. The federal establishment, in short, has not kept pace with population growth. Moreover, national defense and the postal service account for 60 percent of federal employment.

Why then the widespread idea about the remorseless growth of government? It is partly because in the 1960s the national government assumed new and intrusive functions: affirmative action in civil rights, environmental protection, safety and health in the workplace, community organization, legal aid to the poor. Although this enlargement of the federal regulatory role was accompanied by marked growth in the size of government on all levels, the expansion has taken place primarily in state and local government. Whereas the federal force increased by only 27 percent in the 30 years after 1950, the state and local government force increased by an astonishing 212 percent.

Despite the statistics, the conviction flourishes in some minds that the national government is a steadily growing behemoth swallowing up the liberties of the people. The foes of Washington prefer local government, feeling it is closer to the people and therefore allegedly more responsive to popular needs. Obviously there is a great deal to be said for settling local questions locally. But local government is characteristically the government of the locally powerful. Historically, the way the locally powerless have won their human and constitutional rights has often been through appeal to the national government. The national government has vindicated racial justice against local bigotry, defended the Bill of Rights against local vigilantism, and protected natural resources against local greed. It has civilized industry and secured the rights of labor organizations. Had the states' rights creed prevailed, there would perhaps still be slavery in the United States.

The national authority, far from diminishing the individual, has given most Americans more personal dignity and liberty than ever before. The individual freedoms destroyed by the increase in national authority have been in the main

11

the freedom to deny black Americans their rights as citizens; the freedom to put small children to work in mills and immigrants in sweatshops; the freedom to pay starvation wages, require barbarous working hours, and permit squalid working conditions; the freedom to deceive in the sale of goods and securities; the freedom to pollute the environment—all freedoms that, one supposes, a civilized nation can readily do without.

"Statements are made," said President John F. Kennedy in 1963, "labelling the Federal Government an outsider, an intruder, an adversary. . . . The United States Government is not a stranger or not an enemy. It is the people of fifty states joining in a national effort. . . . Only a great national effort by a great people working together can explore the mysteries of space, harvest the products at the bottom of the ocean, and mobilize the human, natural, and material resources of our lands."

So an old debate continues. However, Americans are of two minds. When pollsters ask large, spacious questions—Do you think government has become too involved in your lives? Do you think government should stop regulating business?—a sizable majority opposes big government. But when asked specific questions about the practical work of government—Do you favor social security? unemployment compensation? Medicare? health and safety standards in factories? environmental protection? government guarantee of jobs for everyone seeking employment? price and wage controls when inflation threatens?—a sizable majority approves of intervention.

In general, Americans do not want less government. What they want is more efficient government. They want government to do a better job. For a time in the 1970s, with Vietnam and Watergate, Americans lost confidence in the national government. In 1964, more than three-quarters of those polled had thought the national government could be trusted to do right most of the time. By 1980 only one-quarter was prepared to offer such trust. But by 1984 trust in the federal government to manage national affairs had climbed back to 45 percent.

Bureaucracy is a term of abuse. But it is impossible to run any large organization, whether public or private, without a bureaucracy's division of labor and hierarchy of authority. And we live in a world of large organizations. Without bureaucracy modern society would collapse. The problem is not to abolish bureaucracy, but to make it flexible, efficient, and capable of innovation.

Two hundred years after the drafting of the Constitution, Americans still regard government with a mixture of reliance and mistrust—a good combination. Mistrust is the best way to keep government reliable. Informed criticism is the means of correcting governmental inefficiency, incompetence, and arbitrariness; that is, of best enabling government to play its essential role. For without government, we cannot attain the goals of the Founding Fathers. Without an understanding of government, we cannot have the informed criticism that makes government do the job right. It is the duty of every American citizen to know our government—which is what this series is all about.

A late-19th-century woodcut entitled The Flying Man *depicts French artist Restif de La Bretonne's designs for a set of wings and a parachute. Such fanciful conceptions of flight persisted well past the turn of the century, until the Wright brothers stunned the world with a machine that could truly fly.*

ONE

Forerunners of the U.S. Air Force

Now a sizable part of America's defenses and the largest airborne military detachment in the world, the Department of the Air Force can trace its origin to mankind's earliest dreams of flight. Seemingly bound forever to the earth's surface, humans at first could only gaze with envy at the freedom of soaring birds and let their imagination roam into that realm where they could not venture themselves.

A few people did more than just dream about flight, and their accomplishments led directly to today's concept of air power as a key element of military strategy. The United States and other countries have harnessed these inventions and strategies to great effect. Today's Department of the Air Force is a mighty military force of 575,603 men and women; 7,129 aircraft; and 1,000 long-range nuclear missiles. The size of this contingent of people and machinery, as of 1988, is all the more remarkable because the U.S. Air Force is scarcely four decades old.

Soaring Aloft

Aviation was born in France on June 5, 1783, when the Montgolfier brothers, Jacques-Étienne and Joseph-Michel, sent aloft the first crude balloon. Their invention, the first to enable mankind to break its earthly bonds, was made of

15

silk, lined with paper, and filled with air heated in an outdoor oven—hardly the materials of a military device. Unmanned and weighing 300 pounds, this first balloon rose about 6,000 feet, and despite the unknown effects on humans of flying at such a height, work immediately began on rigging a balloon capable of carrying a pilot. Hydrogen, offering greater lift, soon replaced heated air.

On October 15 of that same year, Jean-François Pilâtre de Rozier earned his place in history by making the first manned balloon ascension, drifting over Paris for four and a half minutes. The danger of leaving solid ground soon became evident, for Pilâtre de Rozier died two years later when his hydrogen-filled balloon exploded while crossing the English Channel. But the barrier had been broken, and the race was on for man to go ever higher and faster. With or without a passenger, balloons would be the principal weapon of air forces around the world for more than a hundred years. (Hydrogen would be replaced by the nonflammable helium in the 20th century.)

The potential military applications of these achievements did not escape the attention of American statesman and scientist Benjamin Franklin, who had observed these ascensions in his role as U.S. representative to France. In a letter dated November 21, 1783, he wrote that balloons could be used by military forces for several purposes, "such as elevating an engineer to take a view of an enemy's army, works, etc., conveying intelligence into or out of a besieged town, giving signals to distant places, or the like." His ideas were generally ignored or shunted aside as impractical.

Not all Americans scoffed at Franklin's ideas. His own city of Philadelphia, then the capital of the United States, was the scene of the first manned balloon ascension in the New World. Jean-Pierre-François Blanchard, the most renowned of the early French aeronauts, as they were called, accomplished that feat on the morning of January 9, 1793, or 10 years after the Montgolfiers' breakthrough. Looking on was President George Washington, who issued Blanchard a "passport" requesting that anyone who found the aeronaut (who did not speak English) should treat him courteously.

Blanchard made a successful 46-minute, 15-mile trip to what is now Woodbury, New Jersey, where the local farmers were sufficiently impressed by President Washington's passport that they escorted the aeronaut and his balloon back to Philadelphia. He arrived there at 7:00 in the evening and immediately called on the president to thank him for his assistance. The air age had arrived in the country where the airplane and rockets—capable of moon flight—would later be invented.

Benjamin Franklin's proposition that balloons could be used for military purposes languished until 1861, when President Abraham Lincoln ordered the

In September 1783, the Montgolfier brothers again launched their invention—a balloon—from Versailles, France. Two months later, after test-flying another balloon with animals as passengers, they sent aloft the first manned balloon.

creation of a balloon corps during the Civil War. The corps's purpose was to observe Confederate troop movements, an activity now called aerial reconnaissance. Balloons evolved throughout the 19th century, serving chiefly as a means of transportation.

The limitations of balloons in warfare were obvious: They are slow, cumbersome vehicles that are vulnerable to enemy fire. Clearly, a more efficient type of vehicle was needed. That vehicle, the airplane, owes its existence to two breakthroughs that occurred late in the 19th century. One was the invention of the internal-combustion engine. The other was the gradual improvement in the science of aerodynamics.

Mechanized Flight

Until 1883, when the German engineer Gottlieb Daimler invented the internal-combustion engine, the most efficient source of power was the large, and heavy, steam engine. Steam engines were well-suited for pulling railroad trains and powering industrial machinery, but proved too heavy for aircraft. Daimler's engine mixed fuel and air inside a cylinder, ignited the mixture, and used the

17

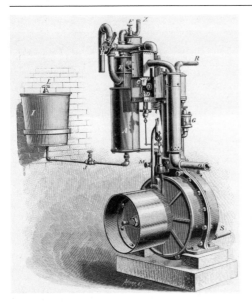

A single-cylinder engine built by the Daimler Motor Company of New York. In 1883, the German engineer Gottlieb Daimler invented the high-speed internal-combustion engine, which mixed fuel and air inside a cylinder and used the energy from exploding gases to drive a piston. Such engines became the principal power source for aircraft during the early 20th century.

resulting explosion to drive a piston. Much lighter than a steam engine, the internal-combustion engine proved remarkably efficient. The same basic principle of internal combustion is still used to power automobiles.

The other great advance, aerodynamics, evolved slowly during the late 19th century as scientists began to realize that birds do not fly simply by flapping their wings. Birds can sustain flight because their wings allow air to flow efficiently over the partially curved surfaces and thus provide what is known as lift. The early aviation pioneers, striving to design their aircraft to obtain the lift that birds acquire naturally, advanced by trial and error. But the trials were short and the errors often fatal: Dozens of innovators died in the course of these trials, including German pioneer Otto Lilienthal, who was killed in a crash in 1896. Lilienthal had begun with work on the glider, an unpowered apparatus that can stay aloft for an extended period of time, but that has little military or commercial value because it is so dependent upon the currents of the wind.

Other pioneers of mechanized flight picked up from there. Lift is not enough; control is also essential to flight. Airplanes have to mimic a bird's natural in-flight flexibility, and they do so through the use of ailerons, movable parts on the trailing edge of the wings. One person who helped develop this technology was Samuel P. Langley, the head of the Smithsonian Institution in Washington, D.C., and a noted astronomer as well. Around 1900 Langley joined with Alexander Graham Bell (more celebrated for his work on the telephone) and

Glenn Curtiss (whose company built motorcycles and later airplane engines) in solving the problem of a flying machine's stability of balance. Each of them contributed in some way to the addition of ailerons on a plane's wings, giving it the needed control. Yet Langley, too, suffered a series of embarrassing setbacks. In 1903 his mechanically propelled machines failed twice in test flights, and his funding soon ran out.

Two little-known bicycle makers in Dayton, Ohio, Wilbur and Orville Wright, thought they had a better approach to the whole idea of flight—and in the process they were probably more responsible than anybody else for the creation of today's U.S. Air Force. Why not put wings of different shapes into

A replica of the original wind tunnel invented by the Wright brothers in 1900. The Wright brothers put wings of different shapes into a box and blew air over them to see which shapes provided the most lift. The wind tunnel continues to be widely used for testing new airplanes before pilots undertake potentially dangerous flight tests.

a box, they reasoned, and blow air over them to see which shapes provided the most lift? Thus in 1900 the wind tunnel was born, still the principal method for testing new airplane designs before undertaking potentially dangerous flight tests.

The Wrights tested more than 200 types of wing surfaces in their crude wind tunnel before they were ready to risk a manned flight. They took their flying machine to Kill Devil Hill near Kitty Hawk, North Carolina, because the U.S. Weather Bureau told them it was one of the windiest places in the country. After many experimental flights aboard gliders, on the morning of December 17, 1903, they flipped a coin to see who would have the honor of making the first flight powered by a machine. Orville, the younger brother, won the toss. He then climbed aboard the *Flyer*, a biplane (having 2 sets of wings) with 2 propellers chain-driven by an internal-combustion motor; and flew it a distance of 120 feet in 12 seconds. In doing so, he ushered in the modern age of aviation.

This period of rapid advances in flight, from the Montgolfier brothers to the Wright brothers, laid the foundation for a revolution in warfare. Until the

On December 17, 1903, at Kill Devil Hill near Kitty Hawk, North Carolina, Orville Wright became the first person to successfully fly a self-propelled heavier-than-air machine—a biplane called the Flyer. *While his brother Wilbur watched, Orville flew 120 feet in 12 seconds and ushered in the modern age of aviation.*

advent of flying machines, war, whether on land or at sea, had essentially been a struggle on the two-dimensional surface of the earth. Aviation gave it a third, vertical dimension.

The Army's Early Role

As military aviation evolved from balloons to propeller-driven aircraft and then to today's jet aircraft, the responsibility for operating these forces was assigned to units of the U.S. Army. The first of these was the Aeronautical Division established within the Army Signal Corps in 1907 with a total force of just three servicemen. During World War I this grew to become the Army Air Service, nearly 200,000 strong.

The army, in parallel with the navy, continued to advance American military aviation after World War I. The Army dirigible (a balloon with an internal framework of wires to help it hold its shape) stayed in service, as did the navy's Curtiss "Jenny" (the nickname of the JN-4), both aircraft also making the switch from combat service to barnstorming and civil transport.

During World War II, the army built up a powerful force of more than 2 million people in its Army Air Forces. This organization played a key role in defeating the Nazi German forces that had overrun Europe and in recapturing territory in Asia and the Pacific Ocean conquered by Japanese forces.

Throughout this period the aviators had sought a separate military service of their own, independent of the army. Finally, on September 18, 1947, after ratification by Congress, President Harry Truman signed the National Security Act into law. The bill created today's Department of the Air Force.

This new, independent military service has taken on increased importance in the present age of missiles and spacecraft. The air force continues to employ its aircraft to protect the United States against enemy attack by air and to support the army and navy by defending them against enemy aircraft overseas. But the air force has also assumed new offensive responsibilities, should they be needed, to operate the strategic missiles and bombers intended to prevent nuclear war by the threat of retaliation. Other responsibilities include operation of the reconnaissance and communications satellites that are also needed for national defense.

As the nature of warfare changes, the mission of the Department of the Air Force is changing with it. As a highly trained military service, it is capable of deploying some of the most modern weapons in the world. At the direction of the president and Congress it stands ready to use these resources to respond to any threats to national security.

*An American aviator poses in front of his plane during World War I.
Although the army had an aviation section in the Signal Corps, it did not
have a full-fledged air force until 1918, when the War Department set up the
Air Service to train and organize aviation units.*

TWO

From Balloons
to Bombers

When one looks at the sleek, electronic- and computer-equipped jet aircraft of today's U.S. Air Force, it is hard to imagine that this huge military force was born during the early days of the Civil War with just two balloons. The date was April 19, 1861, exactly a week after the first shots of that war were fired at Fort Sumter, South Carolina. Two members of a volunteer regiment from Rhode Island had rushed to Washington, D.C., to offer their services—and their balloons—to the Union cause.

The two were James Allen, who had been experimenting with balloons on his own for four years, and a friend, Dr. William Helme, a dentist. The government accepted their offer, and on June 9 they inflated one of their balloons at a city gas main in downtown Washington and made their first test flight from a farm one mile north of the Capitol building. The test was successful, so the two rushed their balloons out to the nearby Virginia countryside in an attempt to observe the Confederate troops gathering near the railroad junction at Manassas.

Unfortunately, both balloons were destroyed during attempts to launch them and the cause of military ballooning was temporarily set back. On June 12 another American who had been independently experimenting with balloons, John Wise, offered to build a new balloon in 2 weeks at a cost of $850. The army accepted his offer, and on July 1 he became the first military balloonist in the Union forces. Wise had his balloon ready in time for the first battle of

Manassas on July 20, but it too was damaged before he could get it into the air. The Union troops were driven back to Washington. But Wise was able to repair his balloon and, observing the Confederates' advance on the ground below, he relayed information about their position to Union defenders. His balloon got loose as he was preparing to launch it again, however, and had to be shot down to prevent it from falling into Confederate hands. The army blamed him for the accident, and Wise quit his career as a military balloonist and went home to Pennsylvania.

The Balloon Corps

Despite the failure of the balloons at Manassas, another balloonist, Thaddeus S. C. Lowe, persuaded President Abraham Lincoln to let him try to apply them to warfare. Lincoln agreed, and in September Lowe was named head of the Balloon Corps of the Army of the Potomac. Seven balloons and the aeronauts to fly them were stationed along the Potomac River as part of the defenses around the capital. On September 24 Lowe successfully directed Union artillery fire against Confederate troop positions in Virginia by observing where the shells landed and sending corrections to the gunners via a telegraph wire strung from his balloon. Aeronauts also used mirrors to send signals by flashing them in the sun.

In November 1861 Lowe made a significant contribution to air power: He realized it would be easier to make balloon ascensions from water, where there were no trees to get hung up in, than from land, so he began launching from a navy coal barge, the USS *George Washington Parke Custis*, anchored in the Potomac. Thus did a coal barge become the world's first crude aircraft carrier.

The Confederates tried to establish a balloon corps of their own, but they could get only enough material (by sewing together women's silk dresses) to make one balloon. They also launched their balloon from a steamer, but the balloon was captured by Union forces when the boat ran aground.

In the end Lowe did not do much better than his predecessors. When he and his balloon were transferred from the Quartermaster Corps to the Corps of Engineers on April 7, 1863, the army's chief engineer reduced Lowe's pay from $10 to $6 a day. Lowe protested and refused to take any pay at all until the army restored his previous rate, but he stayed on for a month without pay and then quit.

After only two years of existence, the balloon corps was disbanded in June 1863. It had served a kind of sentry duty and provided reconnaissance help, but its overall value in the war effort was slight. For two more years the Union

24

From his balloon, the Intrepid, *Professor Thaddeus S. C. Lowe made daily observations of Confederate troop movements for the Union army during the Civil War. Lowe convinced President Abraham Lincoln that balloons could help direct artillery fire against the Confederates; in 1861, President Lincoln named him head of the Balloon Corps of the Army of the Potomac.*

army pressed a ground attack into the South, making use of railroads and canals, and it blockaded the South's coastline with the new ironclad ships. The potential for American military air power would go unexploited for another 30 years.

The lessons of the American Civil War did not go unnoticed in Europe, however, and all the great powers—Britain, France, Germany, Italy, Russia, and Spain—established balloon corps as branches of their armies. One American, Adolphus Greely, who had enlisted as a private in the Union army in 1861 while still a teenager, also remembered the role that balloons had played in the Civil War.

Greely eventually rose to the rank of major general, having served as chief signal officer of the army from 1887 to 1906. He can truly be called the father of military aviation in the United States. When, on October 1, 1890, Congress gave the Signal Corps the duty of collecting and transmitting information for the army, Greely interpreted that responsibility to include aviation. The following year he sent Lieutenant William Glassford to France to study military balloon developments for a year and to buy one balloon for the U.S. Army.

Brigadier General Adolphus Greely, who was later promoted to major general, served as the army's chief signal officer from 1887 to 1906 and was responsible for collecting and transmitting information for the army. Greely, known as the father of military aviation in the United States, was the driving force behind the establishment of a balloon section within the Signal Corps in the 1890s.

The Signal Corps balloon was used in the July 1898 attack on San Juan Hill during the Spanish-American War. The army's balloonists observed Spanish troop movements during the fighting and are credited with finding a trail up the hill, which enabled American forces to win the important battle.

Glassford did so, and in 1892 a balloon section was established within the Signal Corps. America's air power consisted of one balloon, one army lieutenant to fly it, and a sergeant, William Ivy, who, with his wife's help, kept it repaired.

That was still all the air power the United States had when the Spanish-American War broke out in 1898. The army's one balloon was shipped to Cuba on June 28. Three days later it was used to observe Spanish troop movements during the battle of San Juan Hill, and the army balloonists are credited with finding a trail up the hill that enabled American forces to win the decisive battle. The balloon was so badly damaged by enemy fire that it could not be repaired; by the end of the war American air power was once again back down to zero.

The Wright Brothers' "Air Machines"

When World War I broke out in August 1914 the United States was better prepared, though not by much. The army had established an Aeronautical Division within the Signal Corps on August 1, 1907, to take "charge of all matters pertaining to military ballooning, air machines, and all kindred subjects." The new organization ordered a dirigible balloon and the first of the new heavier-than-air "air machines."

On July 29, 1909, Orville Wright demonstrates the airplane that he and his brother built for a government design competition at Fort Myer, Virginia. One month later, army officials accepted the Wright brothers' airplane, which flew at a speed of 42½ miles per hour.

In December of that year the Aeronautical Division published the specifications of the heavier-than-air flying machine it intended to buy. The airplane was required to reach a speed of 40 miles per hour, carry 2 persons with a combined weight of 350 pounds, carry enough fuel to fly for at least 125 miles, and stay in the air for an hour.

The two bicycle makers from Dayton, Ohio, Orville and Wilbur Wright, had been perfecting their flying machine ever since their pioneering flight at Kitty Hawk in 1903. Now, they were confident they could win the Aeronautical Division's competition. A handful of other enterprising aeronauts had similar ambitions, but in the end the Wrights' bid of $25,000 and their promise to deliver the airplane in 200 days won it. They signed a contract with the army on February 10, 1908, and delivered the improved Wright *Flyer* on August 20.

The first test flight, on September 17, ended in tragedy when Lieutenant Thomas E. Selfridge, riding as a passenger with Orville Wright, was killed. The plane crashed from an altitude of about 125 feet when a propeller and rudder wire broke. Selfridge became the first American officer to lose his life in an aircraft accident, and Wright's injuries confined him to a hospital for two months. The army continued the tests, however, and a year later, on August 2, 1909, it officially accepted the aircraft. The Wright brothers got their $25,000—plus a $5,000 bonus because the aircraft reached a speed of 42½ miles per hour.

For the next five years military aviation made only modest progress in the United States. The Aeronautical Division was upgraded to the Aviation Section of the Signal Corps on July 18, 1914, just a month before the first battles of World War I broke out in Europe. By then the airborne forces of the United States included 1 dirigible and 24 airplanes. Of those, 10 had been destroyed in training accidents; 12 men were killed along the way.

The 1st Aero Squadron

Although the United States did not enter the war until April 1917, the fledgling air force had seen its first action the previous year during a brief conflict with Mexico. On March 8, 1916, a gang led by Mexican bandit and revolutionary Francisco "Pancho" Villa raided Columbus, New Mexico, killing 17 Americans. The 1st Aero Squadron, based at Fort Sam Houston in Texas, was rushed into duty to hunt for the bandits. The aviators were able to facilitate communication

A U.S. Army Signal Corps balloon in Des Moines, Iowa, in 1909. The Aeronautical Division, established on August 1, 1907, operated the balloon.

between the army's ground forces, but all eight aircraft used in the expedition suffered from lack of maintenance, and in any case they proved to be ill suited for military service over mountainous terrain. The planes were returned to the base in Texas, deemed unsafe, and destroyed. New planes had been delivered, but the pilots found these unfit as well, and the squadron's tour of duty in Mexico came to a premature and undistinguished end.

The "Knights of the Air" Go to War

World War I marked a turning point in the history of warfare. For thousands of years, land battles had been fought by the foot soldiers of the infantry and the horse-mounted soldiers of the cavalry. Now, armies made extensive use of weaponry only hinted at during the American Civil War: armored vehicles, more accurate rapid-firing guns, and aircraft.

Just as the balloons had been used, military aircraft were first employed solely to report on the activities of enemy troops. The idea of using aircraft to attack ground forces—and each other—evolved slowly. In fact, there was initially a sort of gallantry among these "knights of the air." At first they would

In 1918, a Salmson airplane, capable of carrying two passengers, was equipped with a Lewis machine gun. The idea of air combat evolved slowly; however, during World War I Americans realized the importance of air power for offensive maneuvers and mounted machine guns on their aircraft, synchronizing the firing so that the bullets would not hit the propeller.

First Lieutenant Edward V. Rickenbacker of the 94th Aero Squadron, photographed in October 1918, standing by his plane in Moselle, France. Rickenbacker was America's first ace—an aviator who has shot down at least five enemy aircraft. Of the 69 enemy planes that fell victim to the squadron during World War I, 26 were shot down by Rickenbacker.

wave to each other. Before long, however, the pilots were carrying pistols to shoot at one another. Soon the observers in the rear cockpits were firing with rifles. The next logical step was to mount a machine gun on the front of an aircraft, synchronizing it precisely with the engine so that the bullets would not hit the propeller blades. The idea of modern air combat was born.

American air power played only a marginal role in the war, but it may have been enough to tip the scales in favor of the Allied forces of Britain, France, Belgium, the Netherlands, and the United States in repelling the aggression of Germany and Austria-Hungary. The war had been going on for almost three years by the time the United States entered it, and the opposing forces were dug into their trenches for what looked like a long, bloody struggle. The Allies needed help, and they needed it quickly. At the beginning of the war, Germany had 180 warplanes, about as many as France, Britain, and Belgium combined.

The 1st Aero Squadron, eager to improve on its record in Mexico and still the only American air unit with any fighting experience, was the first to answer the call for help. It arrived in Europe in August 1917 and was soon followed by other units, among them the 94th "Hat in the Ring" Squadron, whose most celebrated flyer was Eddie Rickenbacker, America's first ace (an aviator who has shot down at least five enemy aircraft). Despite their lack of experience—and airplanes—the Americans performed well. They bombed important targets behind the lines and are credited with destroying 781 enemy planes and 73 balloons. Rickenbacker's squadron downed 69 of those planes, 26 tallied by the ace himself.

One of the lessons of World War I was that air power could be deployed offensively, not just for reconnaissance and transport. Another lesson was that, for its own protection, a nation needed a separate air force and an aircraft industry to support it. To create a homegrown aircraft industry, Congress established the National Advisory Committee for Aeronautics on March 3, 1915. This organization was given the responsibility for coordinating all the aeronautical research that was scattered around the country—research carried out by both the military and the commercial aircraft industry. The committee performed that job for more than 40 years until it was absorbed into the National Aeronautics and Space Administration (NASA) on October 1, 1958. NASA continues the aeronautical research for both commercial and military aviation that the committee began during the early days of aviation.

The United States then took the critical step of establishing a full-scale air force on May 20, 1918, when it removed the Aviation Section from the Signal Corps. The new name was Air Service, U.S. Army. The service was not an independent military air arm like Britain's Royal Air Force (RAF), which was established just two weeks later, on June 6, 1918. Still a little behind the European system in many ways, the Air Service, as part of the army, had to compete with the infantry and cavalry for funding and prestige.

Aircraft production in the United States began to advance as well. Starting with a capacity of only a few planes in 1913, it soared to 260 aircraft a week by the time the fighting stopped with the armistice of November 11, 1918. Total U.S. production during the war has been estimated at more than 11,000 aircraft, but fewer than 200 of them were ever used in combat. The American aviators had to depend on other countries, mostly Britain and France, to supply their aircraft—about 5,000 during the war.

World War I had not been, as was hoped at the time, the "war to end all wars." An uneasy peace was to continue for another 20 years as the former warring countries built up their stock of weapons, and waited for new alliances to set. The U.S. Army and Navy, confident that they were protected by vast oceans on either side of the country, quickly reduced all their military forces.

In July 1918, Curtiss airplanes are assembled in a factory in Bristol, England. Although the United States began to increase its production of airplanes during the war, it still depended heavily on Britain and France for the manufacture and supply of approximately 5,000 military aircraft.

Orders for 13,000 warplanes were canceled within days after the armistice was signed. Scientists in Germany, a country forced by treaty to admit guilt for starting the First World War and barred from rearming, continued to devise aeronautic improvements.

Billy Mitchell's Rough Ride

There were a few strong supporters of American air power. The most famous of them was General Billy Mitchell, one of the first aviators to serve in the U.S. Army as a major. He made his first flights in 1916, during World War I, and quickly became convinced that an aircraft could sink any surface ship. Two years later, as assistant chief of the Air Service, he demanded a chance to demonstrate the utility of strategic bombardment from above.

The decisive role of aircraft at two battles in France in 1918, at Saint-Mihiel and Ardennes, had advanced Mitchell's case. The proof came after the war, in

Colonel Billy Mitchell (far right), a World War I aviator and an outspoken advocate of air power and a strong, independent air force, was court-martialed for insubordination in 1925. Mitchell had criticized the army and the navy for not fully utilizing air power in the nation's defense.

July 1921, when his aircraft successfully bombed and sank four captured (unmanned) German warships—a submarine, a destroyer, a cruiser, and a battleship—in Chesapeake Bay. Navy officers were visibly shaken when the last ship, believed to be impregnable to anything but the biggest navy guns, went down in just minutes. Still the military authorities would not listen to Mitchell's pleas for air power, so he took his case to the public, charging the army and navy with "incompetency, criminal negligence, and almost treasonable administration of the national defense."

These words, predictably, got him into trouble. In 1925 Mitchell was ordered to come to Washington and stand trial before a court-martial. The trial, lasting from October 25 to December 17, gave him the public forum he had been seeking to warn the country of the dangers of overlooking air power. Mitchell was found guilty of insubordination and suspended from duty for five years. He reacted by resigning from the army, and continued his crusade as a private citizen. The combination of the trial's publicity and his conspicuous advocacy—his articles in the *Saturday Evening Post* and his book *Winged Defense* stated the case forcefully—compelled the authorities to pay heed.

Congress responded to his claims by ordering a series of studies, which led to the passage of the Air Corps Act of July 2, 1926. This law further strengthened the independent status of military aviation and recommended that the organization keep a force of 1,800 warplanes at the ready to protect the country. The Army Air Corps, as it was known, was further strengthened in 1935 when Congress voted to give the corps its own general headquarters (GHQ). The GHQ, located near Norfolk, Virginia, at Langley Field (named after aviation pioneer Samuel P. Langley), took over responsibility for all the army's military aviation activities. For the first time, the aviators were in control and could compete with the other branches of the army for necessary funds. The navy, meanwhile, maintained a separate air arm (which never did become an independent service) to protect its ships at sea.

In 1918, Postmaster Thomas Patten (left) of New York hands a bag of mail to Lieutenant Torrey Webb of the Signal Corps, moments before Webb's plane is to leave Belmont Park, New York, for Washington, D.C. The first pilots to deliver airmail for the Post Office Department were army pilots; in 1926, the Post Office Department contracted out the work to private companies.

Civilian Contributions

During and after World War I, the growth of commercial aviation also contributed to the future of air power in the United States. At the time of the armistice signed in Versailles, there were 20,000 trained military pilots—and no jobs for them where they could use their new skills. The Army Signal Corps had begun experimenting with the use of airplanes to deliver the mail in May 1918. The first routes, from Washington to New York by way of Philadelphia, were slowly extended across the country. In 1926 the army turned the job over to the Post Office Department, which contracted with private companies to deliver mail. These companies soon began taking passengers along too, and the forerunners of today's airlines were born.

Other former military pilots found work as what were called "barnstormers." These were a group of daredevil pilots who put on air shows at carnivals and county fairs. In addition to their thrilling aerobatics, the barnstormers earned a living by taking passengers for rides or teaching them how to fly. The barnstormers, with their white scarves and leather jackets, became popular heroes. They kindled a national interest in aviation, in the process ensuring that, if war were to break out again, the United States would have the airplanes and aviators to fight it.

Perhaps the best-known barnstormer of all was Charles Lindbergh, who electrified the world with the completion of a solo nonstop flight—lasting more than 33 hours—from New York to Paris on May 21, 1927. Others had flown the Atlantic, but none had done it alone, and the daring feat earned him worldwide fame as "the lone eagle." He spent many years thereafter as a consultant to aircraft companies, and flew 50 missions against Japan in World War II.

That war, a decade in the making, and the great strides being made in aeronautics simultaneously helped usher in a new kind of warfare. Transatlantic and transpacific flights were common by the mid-1930s, and the designs of planes that carried great loads of cargo or mail were easily convertible to military purposes. Another approach to flight was taking shape, too. In 1926, an American, Robert Goddard, successfully tested the first liquid-fueled rocket. His early work, during World War I, had been supported by the government, yet the first breakthroughs in rocket science went mostly unexploited. German scientists picked up from there, utilizing small rockets as weapons against British towns during World War II. After the war, harnessed to airplanes, this technology would revolutionize flight and warfare.

Charles Lindbergh flies the Spirit of St. Louis *from Croydon Aerodrome in London to Gosport, England, following the completion of his 33-hour nonstop flight from New York to Paris on May 21, 1927. Lindbergh, the first pilot to fly solo across the Atlantic, became a national hero in the United States.*

For now, however, the aircraft that had proven useful in Mexico and France—and for civil aviation—would get the call for the approaching war in Europe. If the U.S. government and the military services had been somewhat slow to embrace the latest developments in technology during the 1920s and 1930s, they would be quick to put America's greater strength—industrial capacity—to work. And out of the necessity of fighting a war would come further invention.

Wings for the Bell Airacobra aircraft under construction in October 1941. The Airacobra was one of the most technologically advanced designs of its time—it had a tricycle undercarriage and its engine was located behind the pilot, unlike many planes in which the engine was mounted in front. Military pilots, especially those in Britain's Royal Air Force, found the aircraft easy to handle in combat.

THREE

The Bombers
Take Command

Germany began building a mighty military force after Adolf Hitler came to power in 1933. Italy used its air force to conquer defenseless Ethiopia in 1936, while in the Pacific, Japan built up its navy and sought to expand its influence by marching into China in 1937. These three aggressors were to form the Axis powers, and subduing them would shortly require the bloodiest war in human history. Germany and Italy even got to test their newest aircraft models in support of the fascist side during the Spanish civil war (1936–39), when aerial bombing first proved to be a lethal and decisive tactic. The oceans that had protected America for centuries no longer seemed to be a safeguard.

Once again Billy Mitchell sounded the alarm. Even in the 1920s he had accurately predicted that Japan would attack the United States on a Sunday morning. Then in 1935 he pleaded with President Franklin Roosevelt to prepare for what Mitchell was convinced would be a global war. The United States could not rely on purely defensive measures and would need air power to take that war to the enemy, he reasoned.

Prompted either by Mitchell's appeal or the aggressive moves of the Axis powers, in 1935 the army did proceed with the development of the 4-engine B-17 Flying Fortress. This bomber would later take the war to the German heartland and was to prove a major factor in the Allies' victory. It ushered in

The B-17 Flying Fortress, developed by the U.S. Army in 1935, over a city in Germany during World War II. The bomber's performance proved to be a decisive factor in the Allies' victory over the Axis powers—B-17s, along with British and other American long-range bombers, dropped nearly 3 million tons of bombs on German weapons factories.

the concept of strategic bombing, in which military force is applied not only against enemy troops but also against the enemy's war-making abilities. B-17s, in tandem with British and other American long-range bombers, dropped nearly 3 million tons of bombs on German weapons factories.

War came at dawn on September 1, 1939, when Hitler's forces swept into Poland. The Polish defenders were helpless before the 1,400 fighter and bomber aircraft of the Nazis' Luftwaffe (the German air force). After all resistance was crushed the German Wehrmacht (ground forces) occupied the country. Britain and France declared war on Germany two days later.

Although the United States did not enter this war immediately, President Roosevelt persuaded Americans to assist Britain, France, and the other western European countries under attack. The United States would become the "arsenal of democracy," he said, and would provide aircraft and other weapons to the Allies in return for the use of their military bases in the western hemisphere. The program, really a way to pool manpower and resources, was called Lend-Lease—the United States lent weapons in exchange for leases to the bases.

On May 16, 1940, in a speech to a joint session of Congress, the president proposed that American industry produce at least 50,000 warplanes a year. At the time, Congress had permitted the Army Air Corps to have only 5,500 aircraft, and not all of those had been built. By the end of the war the army would have 80,000 aircraft.

From Blitzkrieg to Pearl Harbor

Germany's initial successes with blitzkrieg, or "lightning war," illustrated what air power can—and cannot—do. The light and fast German aircraft were intended mainly to support ground troops in quickly seizing enemy territory; they were not intended for long-range missions during which they might have to defend themselves against fighter aircraft.

This weakness in the Luftwaffe was proven during the Battle of Britain. In August and September 1940 the Luftwaffe tried to crush British resistance in preparation for an invasion by sea. For six weeks Messerschmitt and

On December 10, 1941, British Stirling bombers are loaded with bombs prior to a raid on Germany. Throughout World War II, American and British air forces worked together to cripple Nazi defenses by strategic bombing, in which military force is applied not only against enemy troops but also against the enemy's war-making facilities.

Focke-Wulf dive bombers kept up a punishing attack on Britain's shipping and ports, then its airfields and factories, then its cities—first by day, later by night. But the Royal Air Force, outnumbered by about 3,000 planes to 800, inflicted heavy losses on the Nazis in marathon midair dogfights. The British had secretly developed radar, which enabled them to spot the attacking aircraft from as far as 60 miles and send out their own fighter planes to drive the Luftwaffe back across the English Channel. The success of the British defenders turned the tide of the Nazis' advance across Europe, allowing the United States to prepare for war. Prime Minister Winston Churchill said of Britain's debt to its RAF pilots, "Never have so many owed so much to so few."

Americans, meanwhile, were nervously watching Hitler's conquest of Europe—and the growing power of Japan in the Pacific. On June 21, 1941, Congress once again upgraded the army's air arm, to the Army Air Forces. This wing was placed under the command of General Henry H. "Hap" Arnold, a veteran flyer of World War I who would lead the air force into the jet age.

The war came to the United States on a Sunday morning, December 7, 1941. Before dawn, a Japanese force of 6 aircraft carriers secretly steamed 250 miles north of Hawaii. With their main target the naval base at Pearl Harbor, 360 Japanese warplanes took off from their carriers, and almost totally destroyed the American Pacific Fleet at the docks. Most of the American

---

A veteran World War I flier, General Henry H. ("Hap") Arnold led the air force into the jet age. Congress upgraded the army's Air Division to the Army Air Forces on June 21, 1941, and the wing was placed under General Arnold's command.

The U.S. naval base at Pearl Harbor, Hawaii, bursts into flame after a surprise aerial attack by the Japanese on December 7, 1941. Three hundred sixty Japanese warplanes took off from aircraft carriers and within two hours had completely destroyed most of the American Pacific Fleet docked in the harbor. The next day Congress declared war on Japan.

planes were destroyed on the airstrips, although luckily the three aircraft carriers were out on maneuvers at the time. The attack lasted less than two hours. The next day President Roosevelt, in asking Congress to declare war on Japan, called it "a date which will live in infamy."

Air power had come of age overnight: Between August 1940 and December 1941, aircraft had been almost entirely responsible for saving England from invasion and for wiping out American forces in the Pacific.

The Air Forces Go to War

The United States, in addition to supplying weapons to the Allies, had to gear up to win a war on two fronts. The long-range bombers that the Army Air Corps had begun to develop in 1935 were immediately rushed into production for the Army Air Forces. Flying from bases in England, and protected from enemy aircraft by the new P-38 Lightning and P-51 Mustang fighters, American bombers—the Flying Fortress and the Liberator—proceeded to pound the German attackers into submission. Missions against steel towns in western Germany began in late 1942, meeting stiff resistance.

The Allies gradually took control of the skies and used the advantage to hobble German industrial capacity, flattening the factories, oil fields, and munitions plants in Nazi-occupied territory. The Luftwaffe was never as successful in striking at British industry. In advance of the D-day landings in Normandy, France, beginning June 6, 1944, Allied bombers tried to knock out rail lines, bridges, and airfields near the invasion point. They were successful enough to open a chink in the Nazis' coastal defenses. Thereafter, relentless bombing of German cities—especially Hamburg, Berlin, and Dresden—in 1944 and 1945 led up to the Nazis' surrender on May 8, 1945. Throughout the war in Europe, American and British air forces had cooperated in pursuit of the common goal.

Wrathful God: The B-29

In the Pacific the Allies first had to take back the islands captured by the Japanese in order to attack the Japanese homeland. Although the fighting in Europe was essentially a ground war supported by strategic bombing, the war in the Pacific was a series of battles between naval forces. This required the use of an aircraft carrier, which may be described as a motorized island with a runway, to carry the attacking aircraft as well as additional aircraft to defend itself.

With much bloody fighting, the islands were recaptured one at a time, from the Solomon islands to the Marianas to the Philippines. In the fall of 1943, American bombers based in liberated China began bomb runs on Japan, and by June 1944 the new, longer-range B-29 Superfortress bombers were pounding dozens of Japanese cities in what proved to be the final phase of the war. Even though their situation was now hopeless, with Tokyo virtually defenseless against nightly attacks, the Japanese had sworn to defend their home islands until the last soldier was killed. Their resolve would also mean a heavy death toll for the invading Americans. Military authorities in Washington wanted to avoid this unnecessary bloodshed.

The solution was a secret weapon that had been under development throughout the war and was first tested in New Mexico in July 1945: the atomic bomb. President Harry Truman, who had taken office upon the death of

In 1945, Boeing B-29 Superfortress bombers fly through heavy antiaircraft fire over Nagoya, Japan. In August 1945, two B-29s dropped atomic bombs on the Japanese cities of Hiroshima and Nagasaki, inducing Japan to surrender and thereby ending the war in the Pacific.

President Roosevelt on April 12, 1945, ordered the next A-bomb to be used against the Japanese to force their immediate surrender. On August 6, 1945, the B-29 *Enola Gay* dropped it on the industrial city of Hiroshima. More than half of the city's 320,000 people were killed or wounded, and almost every structure in the center of the city was completely destroyed in a few seconds. Three days later another B-29, called *Bock's Car*, dropped another atomic bomb, on the city of Nagasaki. Japan surrendered on August 14. World War II was over, but a new era was born, an era to be dominated by the devastating power of nuclear weapons.

The United States and its allies had won the costliest war in history, and air power had proven to be a decisive factor in this victory. They had not won peace, however, and the world entered a period that became known as the cold war as most of the major nations of the world aligned themselves with either the United States or the Soviet Union. Although they were allied against the Nazis during World War II, these two countries became adversaries in the aftermath of that war. As each side rebuilt its military forces, air power was to become an even more important factor than it had been during the war. This new age would see the emergence of military jet aircraft capable of flying several times faster than the speed of sound and ballistic missiles that can deliver nuclear warheads anywhere on earth. This would also be the age in which today's United States Air Force would be created.

On February 18, 1981, a Minuteman I intercontinental ballistic missile (ICBM) is launched from Vandenberg Air Force Base in California. The air force developed the solid-fuel-based Minuteman, which can carry 1 or more nuclear warheads and, as of 1989, placed 950 of them in underground silos across the country as part of the "strategic triad" military doctrine.

FOUR

Independent Service in the Jet and Missile Age

T he United States Air Force (USAF) was born, appropriately, in an airplane. The date was July 26, 1947. President Harry Truman had just stepped aboard the presidential plane at National Airport in Washington, D.C., to fly to the bedside of his dying mother in Missouri. Aboard the aircraft he signed a bill passed by Congress the day before that completely reorganized the nation's military structure.

The bill was the National Security Act of 1947, and it created the National Military Establishment, renamed in 1949 the Department of Defense (DOD). It combined all the military services into a single, cabinet-level department controlled by civilians and consisting of three equal branches. The existing War Department was renamed the Department of the Army; the Navy Department was renamed the Department of the Navy, which retained direction of its own aviation units and the Marine Corps; and a new Department of the Air Force was established.

The law took effect on September 18, 1947, and on that date Stuart Symington, formerly assistant secretary of war for air, took the oath of office as the first secretary of the air force. The 300,000 men and women of the

Stuart Symington, former assistant secretary of war for air, became the first secretary of the air force on September 18, 1947. During Secretary Syming- ton's tenure, the air force built up its long-range bomber force and dramati- cally improved the technology for refueling planes in midair.

Army Air Forces were transferred to the new service. General Carl "Tooey" Spaatz, a veteran commander of U.S. bombing forces in World War II, became the air force's first chief of staff. Forty years after the army established an Aeronautical Division within its Signal Corps, the American air forces finally had an independent organization of their own. The act passed by Congress and signed by the president gave the USAF a clear role: It "shall be organized, trained, and equipped primarily for prompt and sustained offensive and defensive air operations."

The First Challenge

The new American air force was to be tested immediately. By 1948 interna- tional tensions mounted as the Soviet Union successively occupied every country in eastern Europe and seemed bent on expanding its influence

The city of West Berlin, encircled by Soviet-dominated East Germany, was blockaded by Soviet forces in 1948–49 in retaliation for the Allies' success in instituting economic reform in the Allied-occupied zones. The Soviets were able to cut all land communication by building roadblocks and stopping railroad trains.

westward. The United States, Canada, and the Western European countries responded by establishing the North Atlantic Treaty Organization (NATO) to resist this aggression.

Not only Europe was divided by this "iron curtain." Around the world, most countries cast their lot with either the capitalist West or the communist East, and the two armed camps prepared for the possibility of a third world war. By 1949 NATO's forces included 12 nations (France is a member but does not participate militarily), with the U.S. forces predominant among them.

Caught behind the iron curtain in Europe were the 2 million inhabitants of West Berlin, a city surrounded by Soviet-dominated East Germany. At 6:00 on the morning of June 21, 1948, the Soviet forces in East Germany halted all land and water traffic in and out of the city. Their goal was to set up a blockade that would starve the West Berliners into submission.

Within hours the United States responded by assigning the air force the job of resupplying the city by air. Battle-scarred C-47 transport aircraft left over from World War II quickly began flying food and medicine into the besieged city. They delivered 80 tons on the first day, but that was just the beginning. By the time winter came the West Berliners would need 1,500 tons of food, fuel, and other necessities every day to survive.

The Berlin airlift (also called Operation Vittles) was overseen by the Airlift Task Force, composed of army, navy, and air force units; in October the British forces joined in. The supply operation continued for almost a year despite harassment of the cargo planes by Soviet fighter aircraft. By the time the Soviets finally gave up hope of capturing the city and lifted their blockade on May 12, 1949, the rescuers had made 276,926 flights and delivered more than 1.6 million tons of cargo, mostly food and coal. Seventy-five British and American airmen died in the line of duty.

It is doubtful that either side really wanted the blockade to escalate into another shooting war, but political provocation can lead to military confrontation. Yet the Berlin airlift triggered nothing more than skirmishing because it was intended to defend American and NATO interests in purely humanitarian ways. Less than a year after it was established, the USAF had borne a major share of the burden to prevent the cold war from becoming hot. The new service would be tested again less than a year later.

The Korean War: The Jet Age Begins

Once again, war came on a Sunday morning. On June 25, 1950 (just two years after the Soviet blockade of West Berlin), Communist forces from North Korea poured over the border into South Korea, which was allied with the United States. President Truman reacted immediately by ordering General Douglas

A North Korean pilot bails out of his MiG-15 fighter after it was shot down by U.S. Air Force jet pilot Edwin ("Buzz") Aldrin. The Korean War was the first military conflict in which jets were used by both sides.

MacArthur to use all his air and naval forces based in Japan to repel the invasion. On June 27 the United Nations Security Council approved the use of military force—Truman called the counterattack a "police action"—against the aggressors.

The police action took the form of a "limited war" because the goal of the United Nations forces was not to conquer North Korea; the goal was to preserve the independence of South Korea. Military air power would once again prove decisive—in the first war to involve jet aircraft on both sides.

The North Koreans initially had the advantage because their Soviet-built MiG-15 jet fighters were faster than the American F-80s. However, in the first battle between jet fighters, on November 8, 1950, U.S. Air Force lieutenant Russell Brown shot down a MiG-15 and won the honor of recording the first jet-versus-jet victory in history. The air force soon added faster, more maneuverable F-84 Thunderjets and F-86 Saberjets, and these new aircraft enabled the allied forces to take control of the skies. Once this was accomplished, B-29 bombers were able to destroy enemy supply centers, rail and communications networks, and war industries.

But Communist Chinese forces entered the war on November 26, 1950, and allied ground troops were seriously outnumbered. Air power became even more pivotal. For the first time in history, jets were escorting bombers, engaging other jets in aerial combat, and operating in close support of ground forces.

After the war ended with a cease-fire agreement on July 27, 1953, many studies indicated that the air power of the UN-backed forces had been the difference between defeat and the limited victory. The USAF's record in Korea was impressive: more than a thousand enemy aircraft downed, tens of thousands of military targets destroyed. Had the United States been unable to take control in Korea, the studies suggested, fighting might have escalated into a full-scale third world war involving the Soviet Union and other countries.

Rivalry and New Responsibilities

While the new air force was performing its mission with distinction overseas, it was facing a challenge of another sort at home. Military planners concluded that the cold war was likely to drag on for many years, meaning that the United States would have to rearm in order to counter the growing military power of the Soviet Union and its Communist allies. This vast rearming procedure, in turn, led to a rivalry between the air force and the navy over which service would take the lead in defending the nation.

Each service has two principal roles to perform. The navy is charged with keeping the sea lanes open for U.S. warships and cargo-carrying civilian ships and assisting the army and Marine Corps in applying military force ashore. The air force's responsibilities include protecting the country from enemy aircraft and supporting ground troops in battle by attacking enemy air and ground forces. The two services came into conflict over which one should assume control of the strategic forces that would be needed to take any future war deep into the heart of enemy territory.

The rivalry flared up once the United States began rearming a few years after the end of World War II. The navy pushed for building new "super carriers" that could transport attacking aircraft anywhere in the world they were needed. The air force countered with a proposal for a bomber called the B-36, which would be able to fly 10,000 miles on a mission without refueling and would carry the new atomic bombs.

After considerable debate over which service should take the lead role in strategic defense, Congress approved the B-36, and the first operational model was delivered to the air force in 1947. With a wingspan of 230 feet (nearly twice the distance of Orville Wright's first flight in 1903) and a weight of 139 tons, it was by far the largest airplane ever built. But the slow, lumbering B-36s were no match for the new supersonic jet fighters being developed by all the major air forces of the world, and they were retired in 1958. (One is on permanent exhibit at the Air Force Museum near the Wright brothers' hometown of Dayton, Ohio.)

In place of the B-36 the air force developed faster, higher-flying jet bombers. First came the B-47 and B-58, then, in 1954, came the B-52 Stratofortress, which was used in the Vietnam War and which was still flying in the late 1980s. These bombers became a vital piece of the new military strategy that has emerged during the present age of nuclear weapons.

At first, military planners favored bombers because it was believed that a nuclear warhead would always be too large to fit into the nose cone of a missile. Two things, happening concurrently, changed their mind. One, military scientists were able to make use of innovations in electronics technology that enabled them to build superior, smaller, more efficient nuclear warheads that

The Boeing B-52 Stratofortress bomber was developed by the air force in 1954, was used in the Vietnam War, and was still flying in the late 1980s. During the cold war, the B-52 became an important part of the U.S. military strategy, which was to rearm with the most powerful and technologically advanced weaponry in order to counter the growing military power of the Soviet Union and its Communist allies.

could be carried in missiles. Two, Soviet planners were going in the other direction. They were building a new generation of huge rockets that were capable of carrying the Soviets' less efficient but equally deadly warheads. The two superpowers' solutions were different but the result was the same: More bombs of greater megatonnage could be delivered to targets around the globe. The cold war had grown hotter.

Rocketry Comes of Age

Any doubts about the power of the Soviet rockets were laid to rest on October 4, 1957, when the Soviet Union shocked the world by launching its *Sputnik I* satellite into orbit. *Sputnik I*'s purpose was to conduct scientific experiments in space as part of a program known as International Geophysical Year, which involved scientists from many nations. But the launching had implications for military strategy, too. One was the possibility of photo reconnaissance conducted from space. Another was the need to control this new "high ground" of space, in observance of the time-honored principle that elevation (whether from a hilltop or from the air) is an advantage in battle. Yet another implication was purely speculative: Would rockets make airplanes obsolete, just as the

A replica of the satellite Sputnik I *on display in the Moscow Exhibition Hall in 1957. The Soviet Union launched the world's first artificial satellite on October 4, 1957, thus signaling the beginning of the space age.* Sputnik I *also brought about new possibilities for military strategy, such as photo reconnaissance conducted from space.*

54

On February 10, 1960, President Dwight D. Eisenhower visits the Air Force Missile Test Center at Cape Canaveral, Florida. The air force is responsible for land-based missiles; the navy is in charge of submarine-launched missiles.

tank had done to the horse, as motors had done to balloons? The tiny *Sputnik I* satellite measured less than two feet in diameter, yet it jolted Americans into an awareness that they would need new weapons of their own to respond to the Soviets' technological advantage. *Sputnik I* thereby ushered in the missile and space age, which the USAF would have to master.

Of course, the airplane was not made obsolete. What did emerge was a military doctrine that became known as the "strategic triad." It included three different types of nuclear-weapon systems: bombers, long-range missiles launched from land, and long-range missiles launched from submerged submarines at sea. The strategists reasoned that, by distributing its nuclear weapons among three systems, the United States would be less vulnerable to Soviet countermeasures against any one of them. For example, the Soviets theoretically could develop better air defenses in order to neutralize the threat from bombers. Or they could design more accurate missiles capable of attacking U.S. ground-based missiles. Or they might devise better methods of detecting and attacking submarines to knock out the sea-based threat. But considerations of cost, manpower, and tactical synchronization would make it virtually impossible for the Soviets to do all three.

The strategic triad took advantage of the three-dimensional war zone that air power had ushered in, so the air force was destined to play the lead role. Two presidents, Dwight D. Eisenhower (a former army general) and John F. Kennedy (a former navy commander), made the decision to assign the air force the responsibility for the land-based missiles as well as the bombers. The navy would retain its charge over the submarine-launched missiles.

Missiles and Bombers

Even before *Sputnik I* went into orbit, the air force had begun research on a new generation of land-based missiles. They are known as intercontinental ballistic missiles (ICBMs) and are capable of striking targets halfway around the world. The shock of *Sputnik I* gave greater urgency to this research. And when Kennedy won the 1960 presidential election, due in part to his promise to close the "missile gap" that the Soviets had opened up, his administration further accelerated these efforts.

The first American ICBMs used what are known as liquid fuels, kerosene and liquid hydrogen stored at very low temperatures. They were neither as reliable nor as safe as today's missiles, which use a solid propellant (metallic grains embedded in a rubberlike base) that can be stored for many years and still be ready for launch at a moment's notice. These early missiles, the Atlas and the Titan, were later phased out as weapons but were used to launch the first American astronauts into space during NASA's Mercury and Gemini programs between 1961 and 1966. They continue to be used today to launch commercial payloads, such as communications satellites.

In place of the early model ICBMs, the air force developed a new family of more reliable solid-fueled missiles known as the Minuteman ICBM. One thousand of them, each carrying one or more nuclear warheads, are housed in underground silos as part of the strategic triad intended to deter global war. During the 1970s and 1980s the air force developed a new, more powerful solid-fueled missile. Originally known as the MX (which stands for missile experimental) and later renamed the Peacekeeper, these new missiles were ordered into operation by President Ronald Reagan. They, too, are housed in protected underground silos capable of surviving attacks by enemy missiles (except for direct hits) and are beginning to replace some of the Minuteman ICBMs.

The air force has also been developing new bombers to replace the aging B-52s. This program began during the Kennedy administration, was canceled by President Jimmy Carter, and then was revived by President Reagan. The new bomber, known as the B-1, does not fly quite as fast as the speed of sound (neither does the B-52), but it is capable of flying very close to the ground in order to avoid detection by enemy radars. In late 1988 the air force unveiled another new bomber, the B-2, which it had secretly been developing during the previous decade. The B-2 is based on an idea tried in the late 1940s, the "flying wing," but scrapped. The bomber resembles a wing but from above looks something like a boomerang. It is called a *stealth* bomber because its surfaces

The air force unveiled a new bomber, the B-2, in late 1988. The B-2 is also known as the Stealth bomber because its surface is made of materials that absorb the signals of enemy radar, making detection of the plane extremely difficult.

are made of nonmetallic materials that absorb the energy of enemy radar. Thus, it is even more difficult to detect than the B-1.

In addition to carrying nuclear bombs, the bomber component of the air force is equipped with cruise missiles. These are small, unmanned, winged aircraft carried under the wings and in the fuselage of the B-52 and B-1 bombers. The cruise missiles, too, carry nuclear warheads. In the event of a war, the bombers would fly toward enemy territory and release the cruise missiles to fly about the last 2,000 miles toward the targets. In this way the bomber crews would not be endangered by antiaircraft defenses. Also, like the B-1 bombers, the cruise missiles would fly close to the ground to escape detection.

Vietnam: The Limits of Air Power

Following its initial successes during the Berlin airlift and in Korea, the air force once again was called to action after warfare broke out in Southeast Asia in the early 1960s. Presidents Lyndon B. Johnson and Richard M. Nixon attempted

57

to use American air power to stem the tide of North Vietnamese Communist forces that were overrunning South Vietnam and threatening to invade other countries in the region, including Laos and Cambodia. Starting with advisers to the Vietnamese air force, the American commitment steadily increased. In 1965 American warplanes flew their first air-combat missions in support of Vietnamese ground forces.

As the fighting grew in intensity and scope, American B-52 bombers attacked critical military targets in North Vietnam and along supply trails in southern Laos. Unlike the Korean War, however, this was principally a ground war in which superior American air power would not prove to be decisive. The war-making capabilities of the Communist forces were too widely scattered to be appreciably weakened from the air. In another realm, the South Vietnamese government proved to be so corrupt that its own people would not sufficiently support its military activity against the enemy. The government's corruption also turned many Americans against what they considered to be an unwinnable and unjust war. The last American troops left Vietnam in early 1973, to be reassigned to Europe and elsewhere in Asia. Two years later, in April 1975, the war ended with a victory for the Communists, as they marched into South Vietnam's capital of Saigon, and the last U.S. embassy personnel were forced to flee by helicopters from the roof.

The lessons of Korea and Vietnam demonstrated both the value and the limitation of air power. Although strategic bombing effectively destroyed the war-making capabilities of urbanized, industrial countries such as Japan and Germany during World War II, and could again in the future, it proved incapable of dismantling a less-developed nation such as Vietnam in the same way. Guerrilla warfare, in which combatants travel and attack in small groups instead of in massed armies, must chiefly be countered with ground troops. Bombing those soldiers from above, especially when they are able to conceal themselves in the hills or in dense ground cover, can be inefficient and costly. More than 500 U.S. planes were shot down over the 1,500-mile Ho Chi Minh Trail, which was bombed daily in an effort to sever the Communists' supply lines through the jungle. In fact, U.S. aircraft dropped more bomb tonnage on Vietnam than they did during all of World War II, not realizing until too late that the bombing was having little effect.

In addition, pilots and planes now face greater danger than they did in the 1950s. Prototypes of a shoulder-fired rocket launcher, combat tested in the Middle East, Vietnam, and elsewhere, proved so effective against Soviet fighter planes in Afghanistan in the 1980s that the utility of daytime bombing and low-altitude operations is being reexamined. If 2 soldiers with a mounted

A Syrian soldier holds a rocket launcher as he enters an alley in Beirut, Lebanon, during a search for rival Shiite militiamen. Such weapons have the capability to down a $100 million bomber and have had a dramatic effect on air force tactics and future planning.

antiaircraft gun or 1 soldier with a rocket launcher on his shoulder can bring down a $100-million bomber and its pilot, air power becomes a liability because of its expense. Armies driven largely by religious or nationalist fervor can in some situations prevail over armies supported by the latest aircraft.

With the prospect of warfare in underdeveloped nations now a serious concern of American national security, these lessons are being applied by the air force and the other American military services. The people of underdeveloped countries have demonstrated their will to resist domination by the major military powers. As conditions throughout the world change, military strategy will shift to reflect the new balance of power.

The leaders of today's USAF are restructuring their organization to meet these challenges. This emerging structure puts a heavy emphasis on improved levels of training and readiness to respond to current threats. It also relies more on advanced and newly emergent technology to prepare for future threats.

Four A-10 Thunderbolt aircraft of the Air Force Reserve's 47th Tactical Fighter Squadron. One of the air force's principal attack aircraft, the A-10 is used to support ground troops.

FIVE

Today's Air Force

Overall responsibility for management of the Department of the Air Force rests with the secretary of the air force, who is nominated by the president of the United States and approved by the Senate. He is one of three service secretaries who report directly to the secretary of defense. (The other two service secretaries are the secretary of the navy and the secretary of the army). Each service secretary oversees a staff of managers in the Pentagon building across the Potomac River from Washington, D.C., and is responsible for the service's finances and operations.

The service secretaries all have support staffs for such specialized functions as general counsel, legislative liaison, public affairs, small and disadvantaged business utilization, inspector general, and comptroller. The general counsel serves as the service's top legal officer. The legislative liaison staff coordinates activities with Congress, explaining the service's needs and responding to congressional inquiries. Public affairs disseminates information to news media and the public. The small and disadvantaged business staff assists small businesses and minorities in bidding for defense contracts. The inspector general is an in-house watchdog agency that attempts to make sure all employees are obeying the service's work rules and that the USAF is working effectively. The comptroller is the service's chief financial officer and is responsible for budget and accounting procedures.

An aerial view of the Pentagon building, in Arlington, Virginia (across the Potomac River from Washington, D.C.). The Pentagon houses the offices of the Department of Defense, which includes the offices of the secretary of the air force and the air force chief of staff.

The top military officer in the air force is the chief of staff, and every officer and airman reports up a chain of command to him. The chief of staff is also a member of the Joint Chiefs of Staff, a top-level group that coordinates the activities of the military services and advises the president on matters of national security. Other members of this group are the chief of staff of the army, the navy's chief of naval operations, and the commandant of the Marine Corps.

Manpower

The nearly 600,000 officers and enlisted personnel of today's air force (all manpower figures are as of 1988) are on duty throughout the world to maintain the peace. They serve in all 50 states and in 26 foreign countries allied with the United States, among them West Germany, Great Britain, Spain, Italy, Japan, the Philippines, South Korea, and Panama.

About 18 percent of them are officers: 107,000 people, of whom 20,833 are pilots. The others are airmen (a term used for both enlisted men and women) and the 4,000 cadets at the Air Force Academy. (See the feature on page 64.)

In addition to these active-duty personnel, the air force employs 218,699 civilians in occupational categories ranging from clerks and managers to engineers and scientists. It also has manpower available to it from those on nonactive duty, the reservists in the Air National Guard and Air Force Reserve. Each of these forces has about 115,000 members, plus another 20,000 in the standby reserve. They are all available for active duty in case of a national emergency.

Thus, the entire air force numbers a little more than 1 million. These servicemen and -women make up about one-fourth of the total of 4 million persons who serve on active duty, in the reserves, or as civilian employees, in the nation's military establishment.

Except in wartime, the members of the Air National Guard and Air Force Reserve are the most publicly visible of the air force's servicemen and -women.

An air force reservist participates in a training exercise for aircraft crash res-cue procedures at Bakalar Air Force Base near Columbus, Indiana. In addi-tion to such exercises, the Air Force Reserve and Air National Guard regularly perform civilian duties, such as helping to fight forest fires and evacuating the victims of natural disasters.

The Air Force Academy

When the air force became an independent service on September 18, 1947, its leaders recognized that it needed a first-class university of its own, similar to the army's U.S. Military Academy at West Point, New York, and the navy's U.S. Naval Academy at Annapolis, Maryland, to train its future officers.

Preliminary studies to establish such a university had begun immediately after World War II—while the air force was still part of the army—but they were delayed by the war in Korea (1950–53). Finally, on April 1, 1954, President Dwight D. Eisenhower signed the legislation establishing the Air Force Academy.

That legislation charged the academy with the mission "to provide instruction and experience to all cadets so they graduate with the knowledge and character essential to leadership and the motivation to become career officers in the U.S. Air Force."

The academy began operations at a temporary location, Lowry Air Force Base near Denver, Colorado, on July 11, 1955, with a class of 306 cadets. In 1958 it moved to its permanent location, an 18,000-acre site in the foothills of the Rocky Mountains, 8 miles north of Colorado Springs. Congress authorized a cadet wing, as the student body is known, of 2,412 men, and the academy reached that level in 1962. In 1964 Congress increased the wing to 4,417 cadets, which is the academy's present size. Women were first admitted to the academy in 1976 and began graduating with the class of 1980.

The curriculum at the Air Force Academy consists of 4 years of academic studies and professional military instruction (about 186 semester hours) leading to a bachelor of science degree.

The academic portion of the curriculum includes studies in the basic

Cadets march in formation during a ceremony at the U.S. Air Force Academy.

sciences, engineering, humanities, and the social sciences. Within this framework, all cadets complete a core curriculum with a balance from the other areas and select additional courses in one or more available majors. They also visit other air force or government installations to participate in various research projects.

Athletics include physical education classes and intramural and intercollegiate sports such as football, basketball, baseball, track and field, gymnastics, tennis, and golf. With few exceptions, all cadets must participate in at least one intramural or intercollegiate sport.

The Cadet Honor Code is the centerpiece of moral and ethical development. Cadets pledge as follows: "We will not lie, steal, or cheat, nor tolerate among us anyone who does." All cadets take a formal course in ethics and receive honor and ethics instruction.

Cadets live in dormitories. A normal weekday begins with reveille at 6:30 A.M., followed by room inspection and breakfast. Classes are held from 8:00 A.M. until noon and then from 1:00 P.M. to 4:00 P.M. Most classes are held in small classrooms and laboratories. The evening meal is followed by an allocated three-hour study period. Taps is sounded at 11:00 P.M..

The cadets are commissioned as air force officers upon graduation and are obligated to serve at least five years on active duty. While at the academy, they receive all food, housing, and medical care at no charge and are given additional money for uniforms, textbooks, and personal expenses. For purposes of pensions and other future benefits, their time at the academy is considered part of their total military service.

Any U.S. citizen between the ages of 17 and 21 is eligible for appointment to the academy provided that he or she is unmarried, has no legal dependents, and is of good moral character. Candidates must also pass qualifying medical examinations, fitness tests, and college entrance examinations. Nominations for admittance are also typically made by members of the Senate and House of Representatives of outstanding young men and women among their constituencies.

For information, including preparation and admission procedures, anyone desiring to attend the academy may write to: Director of Admissions, U.S. Air Force Academy, Colorado Springs, Colorado, 80840-5651.

In addition to its academy in Colorado, the air force has two other means for training new officers. The Officer Training School, part of the Air Training Command, is at Lackland Air Force Base, in San Antonio, Texas. The school selects outstanding enlisted personnel for service as officers and graduates about 1,000 new lieutenants each year. Also, most major universities in the United States maintain Reserve Officer Training Corps (ROTC) units, which annually produce about 2,000 new air force lieutenants.

They regularly perform civilian duties such as helping fight forest fires by spraying foam or dropping sand on the flames from above; airlifting medicine and other emergency supplies to the victims of earthquakes around the world; and evacuating the destitute and injured in the aftermath of floods, tornadoes, and hurricanes.

Reserve units are located throughout the United States and are under the direction of commanders at air force bases in California, Texas, and Georgia. Guard units are also spread throughout the country and are assigned specific tasks to support the Strategic Air Command, Tactical Air Command, Military Airlift Command, and Pacific Air Forces. Reserve units and guard units participate in training exercises with their active-duty counterparts on a regular basis and use many of the same types of aircraft. The air force has long insisted that these organizations are a key part of what it calls the Total Air Force.

The air force's authorized strength is set by Congress, and the figures for 1988 represent a considerable decline from the more than 2 million people who served with the Army Air Forces during the peak years of World War II, in 1943–45. The decline reflects both the lesser needs of peacetime and the changing nature of the air force.

A Better-Trained Force

The greater complexity of the aircraft that now ply the skies—plus the new responsibility for spacecraft and nuclear missiles—dictate the need for an elite, highly trained fighting force. As a result, the air force stresses technical skills, such as electronics and the maintenance of sophisticated systems, for its uniformed and civilian personnel.

These stringent requirements demand that all airmen be high school graduates and that all officers have at least a bachelor's degree. In fact, more than half of the airmen have at least some college education, and about 40 percent of the officers have a master's or doctoral degree. Many of these degree holders studied technical subjects such as computer science, engineering, avionics, or military strategy, whereas others bring to the air force a background in business—accounting, management, systems analysis—or in the humanities—history, foreign languages, or philosophy, for example.

To maintain this elite force the air force has had to pay salaries that are competitive with other occupations. An entering airman receives $699 a month, and this sum can rise as one is promoted. The ranks, in ascending order, are airman basic, airman, airman first class, sergeant/senior airman,

In 1988, General Bernard P. Randolph (center) receives his fourth set of stars from the air force's chief of staff and Randolph's wife. At the time, Randolph was the highest ranking black officer on active duty in the U.S. military.

staff sergeant, technical sergeant, master sergeant, senior master sergeant, and chief master sergeant.

Among commissioned officers, an entering lieutenant receives $1,339 a month, and a general with 12 or more years of service receives $6,041 a month. The career path begins with the rank of second lieutenant and rises in stages to first lieutenant, captain, major, lieutenant colonel, colonel, brigadier general, major general, lieutenant general, and finally, general.

To supplement their compensation, the air force pays many of the living expenses of its service people and their families, and it grants bonuses for hazardous duty and special skills. Civilian pay scales start at $9,811 a year and can run as high as $88,416 for senior civil-service personnel.

Like the other services, the air force has made a concerted effort to recruit women and minorities. This was not always the case. Before World War II the Army Air Corps excluded blacks entirely. Even during the war, in accordance with government policy, black and white servicemen were segregated in separate fighting units. It was not until 1948 that President Truman ordered all the armed forces to be integrated, opening the way for blacks to take leadership roles.

There is still room for improvement. In 1988 only 5 percent of the air force's officers were black, and 17 percent of the airmen were black. Among women the figure was 12 percent of officers and airmen combined.

Paying for Superiority

Although the air force accounts for only one-fourth of the people employed by the military services, it requires a larger share of the defense budget in order to pay the salaries of highly skilled technicians and to purchase the extremely complex equipment that is needed. In the late 1980s the budget for the Department of Defense was about $300 billion annually, of which the air force's share was $100 billion.

Since the end of the Vietnam War, the defense budget has averaged about six percent of the gross national product, which is the sum of all the goods and services produced in the country. Put another way, the annual budget for defense was a little more than 25 percent of the total federal budget, though during the arms buildups initiated by the administration of Ronald Reagan, from 1980–88, that figure reached almost 30 percent several times. On average, the air force's share has been about two percent of the gross national product, or nine percent of the federal budget.

The E-3A Sentry, one of the air force's 33 AWACS (Airborne Warning and Control System) aircraft, is used as a flying command post to direct air and ground forces during combat.

The air force portion of the defense budget is evenly divided into two categories: investment and operations. Under the investment category the 2 principal items are procurement of new aircraft, missiles, and other military equipment, which accounts for more than $30 billion a year; and the research, development, and testing of future weapons, which adds another $15 billion.

Under the category of operating expenses the largest outlays are general-purpose forces to support the other services (about $24 billion), strategic (nuclear) forces ($15 billion), and intelligence and communications ($17 billion). Other categories include airlift, support of Air National Guard and Air Force Reserve forces, supply and maintenance, and training, medical, and other personnel activities.

Old Planes and New

Every year the air force buys about 200 aircraft, and in 1989 it had more than 7,000 available for use. It operates seven main types of aircraft: attack aircraft, bombers, cargo aircraft, aircraft outfitted with special electronic equipment, fighters, helicopters, and trainers.

The principal attack aircraft, which is used to support ground troops, is the A-10. This is a heavily armored aircraft capable of flying at low altitudes. There are about 450 of them in inventory.

The air force also has more than 400 bombers, including the new B-1 that went into production in the 1980s, and the FB-111, built during the early 1970s. However, the main bomber force consists of about 260 B-52s, which now average more than 27 years old—in many cases older than the pilots who fly them. Added to the inventory in 1988 was the B-2 Stealth bomber, the most advanced bomber available.

With the responsibility of transporting troops and equipment for the other services, the air force must also maintain a fleet of cargo aircraft, about 1,600. Nearly 600 of these aircraft are tanker versions used to refuel fighters and bombers in mid-flight.

A special electronics-laden aircraft, designated the E-3, is used as a flying command post to direct air and ground forces during combat. The air force has a fleet of 33 of them, which are also known as the Airborne Warning and Control System, or AWACS, equipped with powerful radar and communications equipment to observe enemy troop movements and advise the ground forces. Another 400 aircraft furnished with special-purpose electronics equipment are used to gather visual information (photographs and television) and to eavesdrop on radio and other communications of hostile forces.

Fighters constitute the largest category of aircraft in the inventory. There are 2,700 of them, and more than half are the F-15 and F-16 high-performance aircraft built in the 1980s; most of the rest are the older F-4s and F-111s, which have an average age of about 17 years. The air force plans to phase out these older planes in the 1990s and replace them with a new aircraft now called the Advanced Tactical Fighter, or ATF. When it goes into service sometime in the mid-1990s the ATF will probably be renamed either the F-22 or F-23. In addition, the air force unveiled its secret F-117 Stealth fighter during 1988, but few details about it have been made public.

The air force maintains a small fleet of about 200 helicopters for special operations, such as search and rescue of air crews lost at sea, but most of the responsibility for operating helicopters rests with the other services.

The complexity, danger, and cost of taking these advanced aircraft up into the sky requires much training and coordination. For this reason, the air force has about 1,600 trainer aircraft used to teach its pilots how to fly and operate aircraft weapon systems.

Command Structure

All of the aircraft named here are organized into squadrons, each with a command structure and supporting personnel and facilities of its own. The number of aircraft per squadron varies, but the average is about 16 per bomber squadron and 18 per fighter squadron. There are nearly 400 squadrons in the entire air force (including air-guard and reserve units) of which about 80 are fighter squadrons, 25 are strategic bomber squadrons, 35 are devoted to aerial refueling of other air force aircraft, and 30 are for airlift.

The air force also operates approximately one thousand nuclear-armed intercontinental ballistic missiles, or ICBMs, as part of the American strategy to maintain a sufficient nuclear-retaliation capability to deter war. At present this consists of 950 of the earlier model Minuteman ICBMs and 50 of the new, larger Peacekeeper missiles (originally called the MX). These missile forces are organized into 20 squadrons.

Out in the field, beyond the headquarters in the Pentagon, the air force is organized into 13 major commands, which account for about 90 percent of all employees of the service. More than two dozen smaller, specialized offices fill out the ranks. In some cases, one base will be home to units from two or more commands.

Air Force Communications Command, located at Scott Air Force Base (AFB), near Belleville, Illinois, is the nerve center of the air force. It provides telephone systems, base communications centers, computer facilities, ground radio and satellite stations, and a worldwide air-traffic control system. This is the air force's most widely dispersed command, in that it has some 49,000 military and 9,000 civilian personnel in 700 units. They are stationed at 440 locations on 5 continents, including all 50 states and 26 foreign countries.

At virtually every air force installation in the world somebody from the communications command serves as the base communications officer. The command operates an air-traffic control system at more than 160 locations and handles more than 10 million aircraft operations annually. The command is also responsible for the engineering and installation of the air force's electronics equipment and maintains a team of troubleshooters ready to travel anywhere in the world on a moment's notice.

Air Force Logistics Command at Wright-Patterson AFB near Dayton, Ohio, employs about 90,000 civilians and 11,000 military personnel to maintain the equipment needed by air force fighting units. It can be thought of as the air force's own warehouse, where all the equipment is stored, repaired as needed, and issued to other air force units.

Military Airlift Command Crisis Action Team personnel monitor telephone switchboards and computer screens at Scott Air Force Base in Belleville, Illinois. The team coordinates airlift logistics for air force units that respond to major crises or disasters.

71

This command manages an inventory of nearly 900,000 aircraft parts and other items at regional storage centers in Utah, California, Oklahoma, Texas, and Georgia. As one of the largest parts and supply operations of any kind in the world, leaders in business and industry often seek out Wright-Patterson's top officers for advice. The base commander during World War II, General Edwin Rawlings, went on to become chairman of the General Mills Corporation, such was his management expertise.

The service's newest command is Air Force Space Command at Peterson AFB, Colorado. It is responsible for warning of a space or missile attack and supporting ground forces from space. It is the largest component of the U.S. Space Command, which includes divisions from the other military services.

The command employs some 8,000 military and civilian personnel at locations in California, Alaska, Massachusetts, Texas, and Greenland, but its main activities are in Colorado. This is the organization that would provide the first warning of an airborne attack against the United States. The information would be relayed to the underground control center known as the Cheyenne

First Lieutenant Kara Hayes is an instructor pilot at Williams Air Force Base in Arizona. Women were first admitted to the Air Force Academy in 1976; in 1988, 12 percent of the air force's officers and enlistees were women.

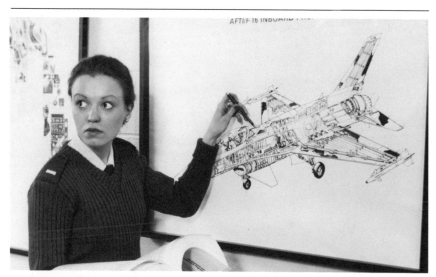

An electrical engineer in the Aeronautical Systems Division at Wright-Patterson Air Force Base near Dayton, Ohio. The base serves as the Air Force Logistics Command center and employs about 90,000 civilians and 11,000 military personnel to maintain the equipment needed by air force fighting units.

Mountain Complex in Colorado, where the commander would immediately notify the president of the United States and the prime minister of Canada.

The space command has the unusual but vital responsibility of tracking nearly 7,000 pieces of space junk in the earth's orbit—man-made objects that have fallen off or been blown off rockets since *Sputnik I* went up in 1957. Technicians make more than 30,000 space observations daily in order to locate these pieces and help communications, weather, and military satellites steer clear of them.

Air Force Systems Command at Andrews AFB, Maryland, outside Washington, D.C., can be thought of as the air force's engineering department. This is the organization that is responsible for developing new weapons systems. It employs approximately 10,000 officers, 13,000 enlisted personnel, and 28,000 civilians, about one-third of whom are in scientific and technical fields such as electronics, aeronautical engineering, computer science, physics, and chemistry. The command currently administers contracts with companies in the defense industry totaling more than $300 billion.

Specific technical activities make it necessary for this command to be subdivided into four major divisions and numerous smaller offices. These

At Wright-Patterson Air Force Base, a crane lifts the tail section of a KC-135 Stratotanker aircraft into position for reattachment after the installation of a new night illuminator system (black painted section at top of tail). The system is designed to improve nighttime aerial refueling capabilities.

include the Space Division in Los Angeles, which is responsible for advancing the technology of future spacecraft; the Electronic Systems Division near Boston, which oversees all the air force's new air- and ground-based electronic equipment; the Aeronautical Systems Division at Wright-Patterson AFB, which has the responsibility for developing new aircraft; and the Armament Division at Eglin AFB, Florida, which develops and tests new missiles, bombs, and other weapons. The command also includes the Air Force Office of Scientific Research at Bolling AFB in Washington, D.C., which sponsors basic research and flight-test facilities for new aircraft and missiles.

Air Training Command at Randolph AFB, Texas, is responsible for recruiting and training all air force officers and airmen. Newcomers to the service are introduced to the air force here before going on, in most cases, to another base or assignment. The command conducts more than 6,000 training courses in more than 350 specialties, such as navigation, jet-engine maintenance, computer science, satellite operations, and fire fighting. About a thousand officers receive their pilot's wings each year at this command's flight schools. The command employs more than 63,000 military and 13,000 civilian personnel.

Air University at Maxwell AFB, Alabama—the equivalent of the air force's own graduate school—supplements the undergraduate programs of the Air Force Academy. Every year about 25,000 military and civilian personnel complete resident classes at one of the university's locations. The primary location is Maxwell AFB, site of the Air War College for senior officers, the Air Command and Staff College for mid-career officers, and the Squadron Officer School. Others study at the Air Force Institute of Technology at Wright-Patterson AFB, which provides graduate-level instruction in science and engineering. Nearly 2,600 military and 1,600 civilian instructors and support personnel make up the Air University staff.

Alaskan Air Command at Elmendorf AFB, Alaska, operates the long-range radar sites and the squadrons of fighter planes needed to protect the United States from an enemy attack originating over the North Pole. This command

An ice- and snow-covered B-1B aircraft at Eglin Air Force Base in Florida encounters simulated arctic weather conditions during environmental testing in the main chamber of the McKinley Climatic Laboratory. The aircraft's major systems are exposed to extremely hot and cold temperatures while in the test chamber.

75

employs nearly 800 officers and more than 6,000 enlisted personnel. Squadrons of F-15 fighters and A-10 attack aircraft stand constantly on alert status, ready to respond to radar warnings of incoming planes or missiles.

Electronic Security Command in San Antonio, Texas, is one of the intelligence centers for the air force. Analysts here gather and organize military intelligence about potential aggressors. They also assist U.S. and allied forces in the ongoing effort to maintain the security of their own computer and communications equipment. This command operates overseas divisions in Germany and Hawaii and subunits throughout Europe and Asia.

Military Airlift Command, Scott AFB, Illinois, is the passenger and cargo airline for the Department of Defense. More than 90,000 military and civilian personnel attached to this command are responsible for operating 1,000 aircraft in 24 countries around the world. In a typical year these planes will carry more than 2 million passengers and half a million tons of cargo. The command also works with commercial airlines in the United States to provide additional airlift capability in case of national emergency. This program is known as the Civil Reserve Air Fleet and involves nearly 400 commercial aircraft. In a related field, the base command operates the Air Weather Service, which is the air force's own weather bureau, to advise pilots of flying conditions.

The Air Command and Staff College of Air University, located at Maxwell Air Force Base in Alabama, is the equivalent of the air force's own graduate school, supplementing the undergraduate programs available at the Air Force Academy. The university offers training in many areas of military studies to officers and senior noncommissioned officers in the air force.

U.S. Marines disembark from a Military Airlift Command Starlifter aircraft during an operation. The airlift command, which is headquartered at Scott Air Force Base, serves as the passenger and cargo airline for the Department of Defense. The more than 90,000 military and civilian personnel attached to this command oversee and operate more than 1,000 aircraft in 24 countries around the world.

Pacific Air Forces at Hickam AFB, Hawaii, is responsible for defending the West Coast of the United States and for maintaining the peace throughout the Pacific region. More than 60,000 military and civilian personnel serve in this capacity at air bases in Hawaii, Japan, Korea, and the Philippines. They operate 300 fighter and attack aircraft, including F-15s, F-16s, F-4s, and A-10s.

The largest command within the air force—more than 121,000 officers, enlisted people, and civilians as well as 15,000 reservists—is the Strategic Air Command at Offutt AFB, Nebraska. It is responsible for operating the strategic bombers and missiles that form one part of the nation's capability to retaliate against nuclear attack; this force is intended to be not an offensive threat but a deterrent to war. Some of the battle and defense plans are devised at the base itself, always in conformity with national policy as dictated by the president, Congress, or the Defense Department. The command's force consists of more than 400 bombers—B-1s, FB-111s, and B-52s—and roughly 1,000 ICBMs. The bombers are supported by more than 600 tanker aircraft for aerial refueling, including aircraft of the Air National Guard and Air Force Reserve. The command also conducts reconnaissance missions with its high-flying SR-71, U-2, and TR-1 aircraft, which gather photographic information. All of the ICBMs are housed in underground silos in Missouri, North Dakota, South Dakota, Wyoming, and Montana.

Members of the Strategic Air Command at Ellsworth Air Force Base in South Dakota wear special protective gear while they participate in an exercise to decontaminate a B-52 Stratofortress aircraft. The Strategic Air Command, the largest command in the air force, manages strategic bombers and missiles.

Tactical Air Command, at Langley AFB, Virginia, is responsible for organizing, training, equipping, and maintaining combat-ready forces for rapid deployment to the front line in case of national emergency. The command works with the army, navy, and Marine Corps to support troops in battle. When mobilized, more than 70,000 members of the Air National Guard and Air Force Reserve, along with their 1,400 aircraft, are assigned to the Tactical Air Command to accomplish its wartime mission. This adds up to more than 4,000 aircraft, or better than half of all the air force's aircraft, and 119,000 people, including civilians. Among the aircraft operated by this command are the F-15, F-16, F-111, and A-10.

The air force has two bases in Panama that operate under the United States Southern Command, a joint command of all three services. Though their presence is comparatively small, numbering about 3,000 of the 10,300 U.S. military personnel stationed there, the air force's role is vital. The southern command is responsible for protecting American interests throughout Latin America, its primary duty being to ensure the security and neutrality of the Panama Canal, a major choke point in geopolitical as well as commercial affairs.

In 1977 the United States signed a treaty handing back control of the canal (which opened in 1913) to Panama after 1999. It is likely, however, that a U.S. military presence will stay on in the Canal Zone to protect Western interests.

The only major air force command with its headquarters located outside the country is United States Air Forces in Europe (USAFE), at Ramstein Air Base, Federal Republic of Germany. It is outside the United States because it fulfills the military responsibilities of America's most important pact with its allies, the North Atlantic Treaty Organization (NATO). Protecting Europe as well as part of North Africa and western Asia, the command maintains units at air bases throughout West Germany and in England, Turkey, Italy, Greece, and Crete.

The USAFE operates 600 tactical aircraft, including A-10s, F-15s, F-111s, and F-16s, and employs 64,000 military men and women and 11,000 civilians. It was originally scheduled to operate ground-launched cruise missiles with nuclear warheads at several European bases, but the Intermediate-range Nuclear Forces (INF) treaty signed by the United States and Soviet Union in 1987 eliminated all of these weapons (those with a range between 300 and 1,000 miles) from Europe. And in 1989 disagreement began to mount within NATO on the future of European-based short-range missiles (those with a range under 300 miles).

Indeed, missiles may not be the only thing canceled. Since the improvement in Soviet-American relations that began with Mikhail Gorbachev's ascent to the USSR's top government post in 1985, diplomatic and military tensions have eased. Public sentiment in Europe, as well as elsewhere in the capitalist and communist worlds, has slowly turned toward a reduction of troops and weapons based in Europe, both nuclear and conventional. In 1989, Spain, for example, ordered NATO forces there to close their bases, coercing them to relocate in Italy. When Gorbachev, in a major speech at the United Nations in December 1988, announced that the Warsaw Pact forces in Eastern Europe (the Soviet Union's main military treaty) would be cut dramatically, 10 NATO commanders started to reassess their own needs, too. It is possible that some American troops, as well as those from other NATO nations, will be withdrawn from the traditional cold war battlefront in West Germany over the coming decade.

If this happens, the scaling down of the air force's commitment in Europe can be seen as a victory for its post–World War II mission: to keep the peace on the most strategically and economically important continent. Whether the force will be redeployed to new potential trouble spots—the Middle East, Latin America, east Asia—will depend in part on its continuing ability to wage or deter war as the need arises.

An artist's rendering of Freedom, *the U.S. space station under development and scheduled for permanent occupancy in orbit by the mid-1990s. In 1987, the air force began working on the rockets that it proposes to use to help launch parts of the space station.*

SIX

Rearming for Peace

From its unexceptional origin within the U.S. Army to its great visibility today as an independent service within the Department of Defense, the air force has grown in stature and responsibility. Once armed only with balloons operating a few hundred feet above the earth's surface, the air force now has a fleet of intercontinental missiles and orbiting spacecraft. The nation's military air arm is still pushing ever farther, ever faster from the bonds of earth. Space, the new frontier, is for the air force the next high frontier.

Along the way several presidents of the United States, at critical times, have lent their support: George Washington for encouraging the science of ballooning in the new nation, Abraham Lincoln for creating the first balloon corps during the Civil War, Franklin Roosevelt for making the United States the "arsenal of democracy" to supply air power to its allies, Harry Truman for approving the legislation that created the independent Department of the Air Force, John Kennedy for promoting the development of a long-range missile force, and Ronald Reagan for proposing the Strategic Defense Initiative—using weapons in space—that may give air warfare an entirely new dimension.

In substance, the mission of the air force is very similar to the role Benjamin Franklin envisioned for air power nearly 200 years ago. The difference is that today this military force is organized into an independent service and is equipped with some of the most modern weapons in the world. Franklin, with the insight he demonstrated in his many other activities, correctly perceived not only the forms that air power would take but also their magnitude on human affairs. Now military aircraft do all the things he predicted. They enable armies to leapfrog their forces over ground-based defenders by delivering troops and bombs behind enemy lines. And they provide an excellent vantage point for viewing enemy troop movements and other military-related activities—so well, in fact, that orbiting spacecraft have been added to maximize that reconnaissance capability.

The importance of air power in maintaining the peace is a lesson learned during the Civil War. That was the first war in American experience to sweep an entire population, rather than just a professional fighting force, into the struggle. Aside from their other war-related efforts, civilians helped make, repair, and launch the balloons, the pilots of which could then observe enemy civilian and troop activities. By giving warfare the extra, vertical dimension, the flying machines that evolved from the early reconnaissance balloons have taken away the security of national borders from the citizens of warring nations. In the present age of nuclear weapons the borders of all countries have become even less secure. First with jet-powered bombers and then with ballistic missiles capable of hitting any target halfway around the earth in 30 minutes, civilian populations are even more in danger of becoming unwilling participants in a war.

SDI: Security or Threat?

Since the two superpowers, the United States and the Soviet Union, developed nuclear weapons in the 1940s, a new relationship between offense and defense has evolved. It is called Mutual Assured Destruction, or MAD for short. It is based on the notion that each side is deterred from launching its destructive weapons by the assurance that enough enemy weapons will survive for a devastating counterattack. No matter which side starts the attack, the risk of such unacceptable destruction is mutual. Thus, the role of nuclear weapons has shifted: Originally considered offensive weapons, by the 1950s they were redefined as having a defensive role—deterring war. As long as American and Soviet technology were roughly equal, the situation would be stable. The concept of MAD may be changing. In 1983 President Reagan proposed what he called a purely defensive system that would use weapons in space to attack the enemy's incoming nuclear missiles. Again, by using the vertical dimension of the air (and, in this case, space), military forces would be sent above the earth's surface to affect the outcome of warfare below. This program is officially called the Strategic Defense Initiative, or SDI, and was nicknamed Star Wars.

SDI was intended to swing the advantage back to the defense. Many analysts, however—both American and Soviet—view this new technology as a potential means with which to create a way to mount a stronger offensive threat. In the view of such critics, SDI is not a defensive system but a destabilizing element in the current balance of power, a technological leap that could touch off a new round in the arms race.

The air force is a major participant in this debate and in the technological research that underpins it. It is cooperating with the army and navy to determine SDI's technical feasibility and, equally important, its affordability. Among the ground rules for an operational SDI system is that it be able to defend itself against an enemy attack and that it cost no more than the additional missiles an attacker would have to make to overwhelm it.

The present SDI studies are focusing on two angles. One, the program needs weapons, such as high-powered lasers and antiballistic missiles, to destroy the nuclear warheads of an attacker. Two, it needs an electronics and computer system to warn the defenders of a missile attack. Because the incoming warheads would likely be accompanied by hundreds—perhaps thousands—of "decoy" warheads meant to fool the defenders' radars into

An air force engineer adjusting a laser at Brooks Air Force Base in Texas. As part of SDI (Strategic Defense Initiative) research, lasers are being considered as a means of destroying the nuclear warheads of attacking missiles.

concluding that they are real nuclear warheads, SDI would require a much more accurate kind of radar. To interpret all this data, the program would need highly advanced computers, on earth and in space, capable of processing vast amounts of information in seconds and of differentiating between the decoy warheads and the real ones.

The SDI program will be in the research stage for several years to come. One of its prototype missiles was tested successfully over the Pacific Ocean in 1984, but the question of whether the entire SDI system will work—thousands of synchronized satellites, perfectly functioning lasers, and the computer programs to control it all—may not be answered until the 21st century.

A New, Advanced Arsenal

The next century's ballistic force is taking shape today in the nation's research and development facilities. New long-range nuclear missiles, such as the Peacekeeper, are beginning to replace the older Minuteman missiles that have protected the United States since the 1960s. An advanced version, nicknamed the Midgetman (which would be moved around the country on trucks or railroad cars in order to make it less vulnerable to enemy attack) is under study.

On another front, a new fighter aircraft employing the most modern electronic systems, the Advanced Tactical Fighter, is due to begin operations in the mid-1990s. Other new weapons based on advanced technology began to enter service in the late 1980s and are expected to be in operation well into the 21st century. These include the B-2 Stealth bomber and F-117 Stealth fighter, so named because they are made of materials that absorb radar signals and are thus more difficult for enemy radar to detect.

Few innovations come without cost, however. Those radar-absorbing materials (one is a plastic composite also found in diving boards, skis, and some household goods) are said to be causing health problems among aviation workers who handle them.

The air force's other roles are also expected to evolve as the nature of warfare evolves. Reflecting this responsibility is its command structure. The Tactical Air Command operates the attack and fighter aircraft needed to protect the United States from enemy attack and to support the ground forces of the army and Marine Corps under battlefield conditions. The Strategic Air Command operates the long-range bombers and missiles intended to deter nuclear war. The Military Airlift Command operates the cargo aircraft used for

In 1970, air force personnel assemble a Minuteman missile in a silo at Cape Kennedy (Cape Canaveral was called Cape Kennedy from 1963 to 1973), Florida. Minuteman missiles have protected the United States since the 1960s; however, in the late 1980s the missiles were being replaced by new long-range missiles, such as the Peacekeeper.

rapidly moving troops and weapons to the scene of conflict and for refueling other aircraft in the air in order to extend their range of operations. The other major air force commands support and coordinate these activities.

Looking Toward Space

A number of leaders in Congress and the aerospace industry have recommended that the air force should finally be given the prime responsibility for operating space vehicles. This role was originally assigned to a civilian organization, the National Aeronautics and Space Administration (NASA), when it was established in 1958. Given its broad scientific goals, however, NASA is considered by many in the defense establishment to be better qualified to perform the research and development for future space missions than to actually operate space systems, many of which will of necessity involve military applications.

During the 1960s the air force tried to put together a space program of its own by developing a winged spacecraft and a small space station. The spacecraft was called the X-20 Dyna-Soar (the name stands for "dynamic soaring"), which would take off like an airplane from a runway on earth, be flown into space by its two-man crew, and land like an airplane. The planned space station, which would have been much smaller than the one NASA plans to develop in the 1990s, was called the Manned Orbiting Laboratory, or MOL.

The two programs were canceled, Dyna-Soar in 1963 and MOL in 1969, because of the financial drain of the Vietnam War on the U.S. military budget. However, many of the ideas from those programs were borrowed by NASA, such as a reusable winged spacecraft and an orbiting research laboratory.

The Aerospace Force?

Although logic might suggest that the air force be the lead military service in this technological new environment, the navy actually bagged many of the firsts during the early days of space exploration, in the 1960s. This situation may change, however, if the air force assumes the responsibility of providing the rockets that will be needed to launch the SDI antimissile systems into orbit around the earth.

NASA's space shuttle, in the opinion of the Defense Department, is not adequate for that ambitious job. The shuttle was originally developed in the 1960s and is limited to little more than 20 tons of usable payload—at a cost of about $3,000 per pound in 1989. The Advanced Launch System (ALS) (see the feature on page 88) may replace the shuttle for the SDI program—and perhaps for other future space missions as well.

In addition to the ALS rocket family, the air force is studying another winged spacecraft that could eventually lead to regularly scheduled flights in space. It is called the X-30 (the X stands for "experimental") and has been nicknamed the Orient Express since President Reagan proposed it in a speech to Congress in 1986. The X-30 would use ordinary airports for takeoffs and landings and could fly either into space or from one point on the earth's surface to another at speeds much greater than today's supersonic transport aircraft. It, too, is due to be operational by the early 21st century, but the operating costs are expected to be much greater than those for the ALS.

One Wave of the Future: Photonics

Key technologies, particularly in electronics, are making possible the aircraft and space vehicles of an aerospace force of the future. More powerful computers on board these vehicles are improving their performance—and making them more reliable so they can be ready for combat at a moment's notice.

One technology that the air force is pioneering is known as photonics, and it may have an even greater impact than electronics did in its day. Photonics is based on the use of light particles (photons), rather than electricity (electrons), to perform many of an aircraft's necessary operational functions. Some of the new aircraft are being designed with optical fibers instead of electrical cables to distribute information within the craft; future planes may use "optical computers" in which data is processed optically instead of electronically to assist the pilot. These photonic systems are lighter, faster, and more powerful and reliable than the electronic ones now in use.

This shift has come about in very short order. Only since the 1960s have electronics been an integral part of a plane's mechanism, and only since the 1970s have electronic computers been available to assist the pilot. The improvements have brought about greater maneuverability at greater speeds, whether the plane is flying in formation or going solo. Now, military aircraft are so complex that the pilots can no longer fly them without a computer's help. Scientists expect that millions of data-processing operations will digest billions of bits of information per second to monitor these craft in flight. The air force is concerned that even these electronically run computers will not be adequate for the still more complex aircraft and spacecraft of the next generation.

Optical fibers manufactured by the Corning Glass Company of New York. The U.S. Air Force is beginning to use optical fibers instead of electrical cables within some of its aircraft to speed up the distribution of information to help the pilot.

ALS: Rockets for Tomorrow

One of the air force's major contributions to space exploration and defense is the development of a new generation of rockets. These rockets, under a program called the Advanced Launch System (ALS), will be capable of placing radars, lasers, satellites, and antimissile weapons in space.

The air force began working on the rockets in 1987 and hopes to conduct the first test flights in 1998. These rockets are scheduled to be in production and ready to launch payloads such as the Strategic Defense Initiative (SDI) system and perhaps parts of the National Aeronautics and Space Administration's (NASA) proposed space station *Freedom* by the year 2000. They would be used for a variety of purposes thereafter.

Each rocket, if development plans reach fruition, will be capable of sending into orbit payloads as heavy as 80 tons. Dividing the cost of the launching by the weight of its cargo, analysts calculate a launch may cost as low as $300 to $500 per pound. This figure is a mere one-tenth of what NASA achieved with the space shuttle. In its regular flights during the 1980s, the space shuttle had a payload limit of about 20 tons, at a cost of more than $3,000 per pound.

A design by Martin Marietta for a main rocket attached to two smaller winged rockets that could be flown back to earth.

The ALS program can cut costs in a number of ways. The vehicles are expected to use lighter materials, more powerful rocket engines, improved electronic flight-control systems, and new techniques for recovering and repairing the main rocket systems. This last feature will allow the rockets to be used more than once.

Reducing costs is not the only objective of the ALS development program. A stepped-up launch schedule would be the other chief benefit. As a measure of how important this factor would be for the SDI program, top officials of the air force's Space Division in Los Angeles estimate that to put the antimissile system into orbit would require 600 rocket launches over a 3-year period. That works out to 1 launch every 44 hours, whereas the space shuttle is limited to about 1 flight every month. The new vehicles would also deliver larger payloads than the shuttle does.

The engines currently on the drawing board would burn a mixture of liquid oxygen and liquid hydrogen, which is the most efficient known chemical rocket fuel. Danger to astronauts will be eliminated because the vehicles could be flown entirely by computers. By flying the vehicles unmanned, the costs of all the systems needed to maintain astronauts in space can also be avoided.

Even if the United States does not proceed with any version of an antimissile system, there are many other possible uses for these new rockets. The air force would become

A General Dynamics design for a partially reusable booster that has a smaller rocket strapped to its side.

the country's main space-transportation organization.

For one, the rockets could be used to launch NASA's space station, which is scheduled to be assembled in orbit during the late 1990s as a research laboratory for scientists from all over the world. For another, the military services could use the new rockets to launch their navigation and reconnaissance satellites, and the National Oceanic and Atmospheric Administration (NOAA) could use them for advanced weather satellites. Even commercial users might want to use them to launch communications satellites.

The ALS rockets are a long way from becoming a reality. But their potential for upgrading air force and civilian space programs in the next century and beyond bears watching.

The limitation of present-day electronic components is their material. The components are made up of silicon microchips smaller than a quarter-inch square, and they will not be able to process information much faster than they do now. The individual elements on the chips, such as transistors, would have to be smaller. Further miniaturization is currently considered impossible, however, because each of those elements is now as small as half a micron (a micron is one-millionth of a meter). For comparison, note that the average human hair is about 100 microns in diameter, or 200 times thicker than one of these chips. If more transistors were packed more tightly, the electricity flowing through them would cause them to overheat, thereby destroying them.

The advantage of photons—because they need no electricity—is that they do not generate any heat. This property makes them attractive for three kinds of computing tasks needed in all aircraft:

1. Sensors, such as radar, to help the pilot navigate during a mission and avoid enemy aircraft.

2. Computers to process the information from the sensors.

3. Communications links to relay data between the sensors and the computers.

Of the three tasks, one is already beginning to be performed by photonic equipment. The routing of information between radars and computers can be handled by optical fibers, thin strands of very pure glass as small as 10 microns in diameter.

Not only do optical fibers require less electricity (just enough to convert the optical signals to electrons for today's computer) than the copper cables they replace, but they carry much more information: 100 million bits a second, instead of 1 million bits. At the air force's Photonics Center near Rome, New York, researchers are studying even more powerful optical fibers capable of transferring 10 billion bits of information every second. Their goal is to provide the expanded communications capabilities they think will be needed for parts of the SDI system and the X-30 Orient Express. An optical fiber data link will also be used in the new Advanced Tactical Fighter.

The next step is to use photonic devices in the aircraft radars so that air force pilots can identify enemy aircraft more quickly and more accurately. The need for this second quality—accuracy—became especially evident in 1988 when navy planes mistakenly shot down an Iranian passenger jet over the Persian Gulf, thinking it was a fighter plane. Scientists at the Photonics Center are working on new devices that retain in memory an image of every enemy aircraft. If the radar spots a plane that matches one of those images, the pilot is immediately alerted. By identifying a hostile plane or simply acknowledging the presence of a nonaggressive one, memory storage of images will be an invaluable asset to a pilot under the stress of combat.

Beyond information routing and radar, air force scientists are looking for ways to build entire computers out of photonic devices. These would work somewhat differently from today's electronic computers, which are really a collection of switches that process information by signaling "1" for on and "0" for off—hence their name, digital computers. Photonic computers would also be digital but would not need the switches that generate most of the heat. Instead, tiny lasers inside the chips would emit a continuous beam of light that would be turned at right angles to perform the switching function. For example, the beam could be turned to the left to represent "1" and to the right for "0." Such chips would process information faster and last longer.

Manning the Skies

Computerization has already changed the way millions of Americans work and play. It changed the way the Department of the Air Force operated long ago—in keeping records, planning battle strategy, repairing and maintaining its aircraft, missiles, and other hardware. Now, with revolutionary scientific applications such as lasers, photonics, and rocket engines setting the tone, the air force will be still further ahead of the civilian scene.

The greater reliance on more highly sophisticated equipment by the aerospace force of the future poses a problem. In some way or another, every new armament is part of an overall goal of maintaining peace. Yet President Reagan suggested that when the technology for the SDI program is ready, the United States will share it with the Soviet Union. How does that possibility affect the air force? The seeming contradiction of arming for peace becomes more complicated when the role of America's allies is added to the formula. Will sharing today's technological secrets with Japan or Germany or Great Britain give these nations an edge that could make the United States vulnerable 50 years down the road?

Whatever the decisions made by governmental leaders, the military services are obliged to perform their tasks to the best of their ability. The Department of the Air Force will demand better-educated men and women to operate and maintain its sophisticated equipment. From the air forces of the past came a rich tradition of bravery and imagination. Building on that tradition, the nation's military air arm will in the future depend on the quality of the education and the technical skills that its leaders and its new recruits bring to their job.

Appendix:
Air Force Museums in the United States

Eighth Air Force Museum
Barksdale Air Force Base, Louisiana
 Portrays the history and development of strategic bombardment
through the history of the 2nd Bombardment Wing, from 1918 to the
present; covers the history of the Eighth Air Force, from 1942 to the
present.

Edward F. Beale Museum
Beale Air Force Base, California
 Profiles the story of E. F. Beale, a daring figure in the Mexican
War (1846–48) and the exploration of the West. Other materials
date from 1800 to the present.

Hangar Nine, Edward H. White II Memorial Museum
Brooks Air Force Base, Texas
 Explains the history of aviation and aerospace medicine.
Contains exhibits concerning the history of the base, artwork, the
"astrochimps" Sam and Enos's space capsules, and medical research
and testing equipment from 1917 to the present.

Castle Air Museum
Castle Air Force Base, California
 Depicts the history of strategic bombardment with primary
emphasis on the activities of the base.

Dyess Air Force Base Museum
Dyess Air Force Base, Texas
 Recounts the development of Dyess AFB and its role during
World War II.

U.S. Air Force Armament Museum
Eglin Air Force Base, Florida
 Exhibits air force armament and delivery systems.

South Dakota Air & Space Museum
Ellsworth Air Force Base, South Dakota
 Collects, preserves, and displays materials relating to the history
of aviation and space exploration as conducted in South Dakota and
the history of the base, the 44th Bomb Wing, the 28th Bomb Wing,
and other USAF groups.

Fairchild Air Force Base Museum
Fairchild Air Force Base, Washington
Depicts the military history of the area of Spokane, Washington, including Fort George Wright (1898–1956), Felts Field (1924–49), Geiger AFB (1940–65), and Fairchild AFB (1942 to present).

Grand Forks Air Force Base Museum
Grand Forks Air Force Base, North Dakota
Portrays the history of the base.

Museum of Flight
Hill Air Force Base, Utah
Portrays the history of Hill AFB and its role in associated maintenance, supply repair, and training functions, and the history of the Ogden Air Logistics Center.

Rescue Memorial Museum
Kirtland Air Force Base, New Mexico
Exhibits memorabilia of historical significance in air force rescue and weather services.

History and Traditions Museum
Lackland Air Force Base, Texas
Exhibits objects significant in the air force's role in the evolution of aerospace flight.

U.S. Air Force Security Police Museum
Lackland Air Force Base, Texas
Preserves the heritage and tradition of the air force security police.

Lowry Heritage Museum
Lowry Air Force Base, Colorado
Interprets the history of Lowry AFB, its antecedents, and the development of aerospace photography.

Fort MacArthur Museum
San Pedro, California
Illustrates the history of the U.S. Air Force in the Los Angeles area and the history of air force systems command.

Malmstrom Air Force Base Museum and Air Park
Malmstrom Air Force Base, Montana
Portrays base history from 1942, when the base was called the Great Falls Army Air Base, through today's missile era.

March Field Museum
March Air Force Base, California
 Depicts the story of March Field.

Silver Wings Aviation Museum
Mather Air Force Base, California
 Exhibits artifacts relevant to flight and the history of navigation.

McChord Air Force Base Museum
McChord Air Force Base, Washington
 Describes the history of the base and the units that served there.

McClellan Aviation Museum
McClellan Air Force Base, California
 Includes the history of McClellan AFB; its construction and
dedication (1839–1939); its role in logistics support prior to and
during World War II (1939–45), during the Korean conflict
(1945–54) and the Vietnam War (1964–74); and the revolution in air
logistics (1974–85).

Minnesota Air Guard Museum
St. Paul, Minnesota
 Preserves the heritage and tradition of the Minnesota Air
National Guard and portrays the history of military aviation in the
state.

Minot Heritage Center
Minot Air Force Base, North Dakota
 Portrays the history of the base and major assigned units.

Air Force Space Museum
Patrick Air Force Base, Florida
 Exhibits rockets, missiles, and other space equipment of the air
force and associated armed services.

Edward J. Peterson Space Command Museum
Peterson Air Force Base, Colorado
 Tells the story of Peterson Field, beginning with its inception in
1942.

Plattsburgh Air Force Base Museum
Plattsburgh Air Force Base, New York
 Relates the history of the base, of the 380th Bomb Wing, and the
military history of the Northeast dating back to the American
Revolution.

Robins Air Force Base Museum of Aviation
Robins Air Force Base, Georgia
Explains the U.S. Air Force's role in aviation at Robins AFB and in the state of Georgia, with emphasis on military aviation and its significance in national defense.

Selfridge Military Air Museum
Selfridge Air National Guard Base, Michigan
Covers the history of Selfridge Field since 1917 and the units stationed there. Exhibits include all branches of the Department of Defense and the U.S. Coast Guard.

Travis Air Force Museum
Travis Air Force Base, California
Depicts the history of the base and of the airlift in the Pacific Ocean region.

Warren Air Force Base Museum
Warren Air Force Base, Wyoming
Portrays the unique history of the oldest continually active air force base. Highlights the history of Fort D. A. Russell/Warren AFB from 1867 to 1947; displays include memorabilia of the 90th Bomb Wing from World War II.

The United States Air Force Museum
Wright-Patterson Air Force Base, Ohio
Depicts the history of the U.S. Air Force.

Department of the Air Force
DEPARTMENT OF DEFENSE

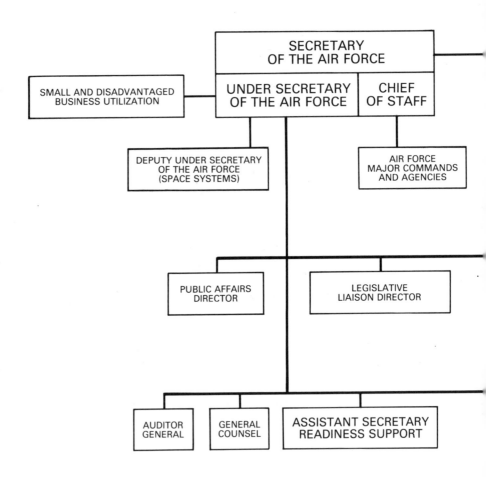

SECRETARY
OF THE AIR FORCE

SMALL AND DISADVANTAGED
BUSINESS UTILIZATION

UNDER SECRETARY
OF THE AIR FORCE

CHIEF
OF STAFF

DEPUTY UNDER SECRETARY
OF THE AIR FORCE
(SPACE SYSTEMS)

AIR FORCE
MAJOR COMMANDS
AND AGENCIES

PUBLIC AFFAIRS
DIRECTOR

LEGISLATIVE
LIAISON DIRECTOR

AUDITOR
GENERAL

GENERAL
COUNSEL

ASSISTANT SECRETARY
READINESS SUPPORT

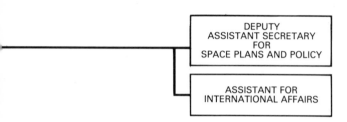

DEPUTY
ASSISTANT SECRETARY
FOR
SPACE PLANS AND POLICY

ASSISTANT FOR
INTERNATIONAL AFFAIRS

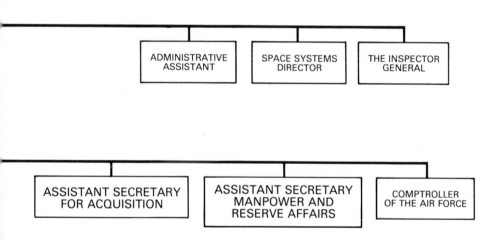

ADMINISTRATIVE
ASSISTANT

SPACE SYSTEMS
DIRECTOR

THE INSPECTOR
GENERAL

ASSISTANT SECRETARY
FOR ACQUISITION

ASSISTANT SECRETARY
MANPOWER AND
RESERVE AFFAIRS

COMPTROLLER
OF THE AIR FORCE

GLOSSARY

Aerodynamics The study of the flow of air and other gases and of the forces acting on bodies moving through these gases.

Ballistic missile A type of missile that is self-propelled during the first part of its flight and then, after its fuel is used up, coasts the rest of the distance to its target.

Barnstormer One who flies an airplane, usually through rural districts, and performs stunts or takes passengers on sight-seeing tours.

Blitzkrieg The German word for "lightning war," a war conducted with great speed and force; a violent surprise attack by massed air forces and mechanized ground forces in close coordination.

Cold war A conflict over ideological differences that leads to rivalry, mistrust, and often open hostility short of violence between two nations or groups of nations. Despite the conflict between the nations, diplomatic relations are usually maintained.

Dirigible A lighter-than-air aircraft having propulsion and steering systems.

Photonics The use of light particles (photons) rather than electricity (electrons) to perform many of an aircraft's necessary operational functions.

Reconnaissance craft An aircraft or vessel used to obtain information about enemy territory and military positions.

Strategic bombing A strategy in which air power is directed not only against enemy troops but also against an enemy's war-making capabilities, such as weapons factories.

Wind tunnel A tunnellike passage through which air is blown at a certain velocity to determine the effects of wind pressure on an object placed in the passage. This device was invented by the Wright brothers and is still widely used for testing new airplanes before pilots make test flights.

SELECTED REFERENCES

Air Force Magazine, "Air Force Almanac 1988." Arlington, VA: Air Force Association, May 1988.

Borklund, C. W. *The Department of Defense.* New York: Praeger, 1968.

Corn, Joseph J. *The Winged Gospel: America's Romance with Aviation, 1900–1950.* New York: Oxford University Press, 1983.

Fagan, George V. *The Air Force Academy.* Boulder, CO: Johnson Books, 1988.

Glines, Carroll V., Jr. *The Compact History of the United States Air Force.* Salem, NH: Ayer, 1979.

Hersey, John. *Hiroshima.* New York: Knopf, 1948.

Higham, Robin. *Air Power: A Concise History.* New York: St. Martin's, 1972.

LeMay, Curtis E., and Bill Yenne. *Superfortress: The Story of the B-29 and American Air Power in World War II.* New York: McGraw-Hill, 1988.

Loosbrock, John F., and Richard M. Skinner. *The Wild Blue: The Story of American Airpower.* New York: Putnam, 1961.

MacCloskey, Monro. *The United States Air Force.* New York: Praeger, 1967.

Nevin, David. *Architects of Air Power.* Alexandria, VA: Time-Life Books, 1981.

Smallwood, William L. *The Air Force Academy Candidate Book.* Litchfield Park, AZ: Beacon Books, 1988.

INDEX

B-2, 56, 57
B-2 Stealth bomber, 56, 69, 84

Carter, Jimmy, 56
Churchill, Winston, 42
Civil Reserve Air Fleet, 76
Civil War, 17, 23, 26, 30, 81, 82
Cold war, 45, 52, 54
Cruise missiles, 57
Curtiss, Glenn, 19

Daimler, Gottlieb, 17
Department of Defense (DOD), 47, 76, 77, 81, 86
   budget of, 68
Dirigibles, 21, 29

Eisenhower, Dwight D., 55
Electronic Security Command, 76
Enola Gay, 45
E-3, 69

FB-111, 69, 77
F-80, 51
F-84 Thunderjets, 51
F-86 Saberjets, 51
F-15, 70, 77, 78, 79
F-4, 70, 77
Fighters, 70. *See also specific names*
1st Aero Squadron, 29–30, 31–32
Flyer, 28
F-111, 70, 78, 79
F-117 Stealth fighter, 84
France, 15, 16, 26, 31, 32, 33, 37, 40, 44, 50
Franklin, Benjamin, 16, 81
F-16, 70, 77, 78, 79

Germany, 26, 31, 33, 39, 40, 41, 44, 58, 91
Glassford, William, 26, 27
Goddard, Robert, 36
Gorbachev, Mikhail, 79

Great Britain, 26, 31, 32, 40, 42, 43, 50, 62, 91
Greely, Adolphus, 26

Helme, William, 23
Hiroshima, Japan, 45
Hitler, Adolf, 39, 40, 42

Intercontinental ballistic missiles (ICBMs), 56, 70, 77, 81, 82
Intermediate-range Nuclear Forces (INF) treaty, 79
Internal-combustion engine, 17–18
International Geophysical Year, 54
Italy, 26, 39, 62
Ivy, William, 27

Japan, 36, 39, 42, 43, 44, 51, 58, 62, 77, 91
Johnson, Lyndon B., 57

Kennedy, John F., 55, 56, 81
Kitty Hawk, North Carolina, 20, 28
Korean War, 50–52, 58

Langley, Samuel P., 18, 19, 35
Lend-Lease, 40
Liberator, 44
Lilienthal, Otto, 18
Lincoln, Abraham, 16, 24, 81
Lindbergh, Charles, 36
Lowe, Thaddeus S. C., 24
Lutfwaffe, 40, 41, 42, 44

MacArthur, Douglas, 50–51
Manned Orbiting Laboratory, 86
Mariana islands, 44
Marine Corps, U.S., 52
Mexico, 29, 30, 31, 37
Midgetman, 84
MiG-15 fighters, 51

as 30 years' experience as a writer and editor specializing in .nology, and national affairs. He has written for numerous , including *Air Force Magazine, The Economist, International eview,* and the *Washington Post* and is the author of *SDI: What Could , Eight Possible Star Wars Scenarios.* He received a B.S. in journalism the University of Illinois and studied at the Industrial College of the .ied Forces, Washington, D.C., and Hunter College, New York.

Arthur M. Schlesinger, jr., served in the White House as special assistant to Presidents Kennedy and Johnson. He is the author of numerous acclaimed works in American history and has twice been awarded the Pulitzer Prize. He taught history at Harvard College for many years and is currently Albert Schweitzer Professor of the Humanities at the City College of New York.